Tariff Schmariff
A Satire Without Borders

Barry Robbins

Dedication

To Pam, my caregiver extraordinaire, without whom this work would not have been possible. Words cannot express my gratitude.

Contents

Preface

$$\Delta\tau_i = \frac{x_i - m_i}{\varepsilon * \varphi * m_i}.$$

FROM THE DESK OF CUSTOMS & BORDER PROTECTION
OFFICIAL INTERNAL MEMO
CLASSIFICATION: PANICKED

TO: All CBP Personnel
FROM: Office of Tariff Implementation
RE: What The Hell Is Happening

As of 9:14 AM today, President Trump has imposed tariffs on practically every country on Earth. No, we don't know why. No, we don't understand the percentages either.

Intelligence suggests the tariff rates were calculated using a combination of:

- Fox News airtime by country

- Trump hotel locations

- Golf tournament results

- Food Trump personally dislikes

- Random number generator (suspected)

We've received no implementation guidelines beyond "collect the money" and "make it huge."

Calculators are being distributed. God help us all.

P.S. Yes, apparently Antarctica's uninhabited islands are included. No, we don't know how to collect tariffs from penguins.

Chapter 1

Germany: Deutschland Deflated

Chancellor Olaf Scholz was midway through his usual breakfast of efficiently designed, precisely measured muesli when his phone vibrated with mechanical German precision. The notification displayed was anything but precise:

"BREAKING: US IMPOSES 28% TARIFF ON GERMAN IMPORTS BECAUSE 'THEIR CARS ARE TOO GOOD AND IT'S UNFAIR'"

Scholz choked on a perfectly engineered oat flake. "*Mein Gott*! Someone get me Robert Habeck immediately!"

Within seven minutes and thirty-two seconds (a new ministry response record), Economy Minister Robert Habeck arrived, his organic hemp briefcase bulging with hastily printed economic impact assessments.

"Chancellor, according to our preliminary analysis, President Trump appears to have calculated our tariff rate by combining the horsepower of a BMW M5, the price of a Wiener schnitzel in Manhattan, and the total number of German goals scored against the US in World Cup history."

Meanwhile in the White House, Trump was explaining his brilliant tariff strategy to assembled reporters while a visibly distressed Treasury Secretary stood nearby clutching what appeared to be a crayon-drawn pie chart.

"Germany has been very, very mean to us on trade. Very mean. They send us these beautiful cars—I love Mercedes, I drive Mercedes, the best cars—but they're too good. They work too well. American cars break down much faster, creating more JOBS for mechanics. It's basic economics, folks."

A reporter from the Wall Street Journal timidly raised her hand. "Mr. President, Germany is one of America's closest allies and—"

"FAKE NEWS!" Trump bellowed, his face achieving a shade of orange previously unknown to science. "Germany started both World Wars AND they're making our cars look bad! Did you know their 'check engine' lights almost NEVER come on? Terrible for the diagnostic industry!"

In Stuttgart, the headquarters of Mercedes-Benz had transformed into a crisis center. CEO Ola Källenius addressed his engineering team, who were all wearing black turtlenecks in mourning.

"We have received a direct communication from the White House," Källenius announced gravely. "They demand we reduce our engineering standards by at least 28% to qualify for tariff exemption. Trump specifically requested that our cars 'break down more American-ly.'"

Head engineer Dieter Müller rose, his face ashen. "But sir, the very concept violates every principle of German engineering! They want us to... to... deliberately design inefficiency?"

"They've sent us specific guidelines," Källenius continued, distributing documents. "All German vehicles must now include a 'minimum breakdown guarantee' ensuring at least three major repairs annually. Dashboards must feature at least seven unexplainable warning lights, and each car must include what they're calling 'patriotic rust zones' designed to corrode within two years."

At BMW's headquarters, executives were hatching a creative solution. "What if," suggested Marketing Director Hannah Weber, "we create 'American Edition' vehicles? Same German engineering inside, but with exterior modifications to appear more... American?"

By morning, blueprints were complete for the BMW "Freedom Eagle Series"—identical to standard models but featuring cup holders large enough for gallon-sized sodas, eagle hood ornaments that screamed "LIBERTY!" when pressed, and decorative exhaust pipes that released artificial coal smoke when idling.

In Berlin, the German Parliament convened an emergency session to address the tariff crisis. The typically stoic chamber erupted into uncharacteristic emotional outbursts, with one representative actually raising his voice slightly and another loosening his tie a full centimeter.

Finance Minister Christian Lindner presented the economic battleplan: "We propose a targeted counter-tariff on American goods specifically selected to impact Trump's personal interests." The list included golf balls (37% tariff), spray tan solution (45% tariff), and Diet Coke (99% tariff).

The German Foreign Office drafted a formal response to Washington so diplomatically scathing it had to be transported in a lead-lined briefcase. It began: "The Federal Republic of Germany acknowledges receipt of your 'tariff notification' calculated with what appears to be mathematics unknown to European civilizat ion..."

Trump, meanwhile, had moved on to threatening the German sausage industry. "These German sausages—they're too perfect, too delicious. American hot dogs should have first priority in American stomachs! From now on, bratwurst must register as foreign meat agents!"

Vice President JD Vance nodded solemnly beside him. "Each perfectly engineered German car that arrives on our shores is basically a four-wheeled Trojan horse filled with efficiency and reliability—values that are fundamentally un-American."

German television aired a special episode of "Heute Show" featuring a mock interview with an American customs official struggling to calculate the tariff on a shipment of Volkswagens: "Let's see... 28% of the sticker price, plus 5% for every cup holder over three, minus 2% if it has one of them funny European horns that goes 'boop-boop' instead of 'honk'..."

As night fell across Germany, emergency lights illuminated automobile factories where engineers worked frantically to develop "tariff-proof" vehicles. The prototype "Amerikanerwagen" featured deliberate manufacturing defects, a maximum speed governor of 55 mph, and an infotainment system that only played "Born in the USA"—ironically, of course.

Chapter 2
France: Macron's Baguette Diplomacy

President Emmanuel Macron was enjoying his morning espresso and precisely seventy-three percent of a pain au chocolat when his phone buzzed with an emergency alert. His face—normally a portrait of calculated serenity—twisted into an expression of such profound Gallic horror that his left eyebrow nearly touched his hairline.

"Mon dieu! TWENTY PERCENT?" he gasped, sending pastry flakes cascading down his immaculately tailored suit. "Someone fetch me the Minister of Sophisticated Outrage immediately!"

Within minutes, the French cabinet assembled in the Élysée Palace's Crisis Room, decorated with portraits of historical figures making dismissive hand gestures. Foreign Minister Jean-Yves Le Drian entered last, dramatically removing his designer sunglasses despite being indoors.

"It appears," Macron announced, pacing with existential purpose, "that President Trump has declared economic war on French culture itself. He has imposed a twenty percent tariff on our exports because—I quote directly—'they make everything sound too fancy and it makes American stuff sound stupid by comparison.'"

Finance Minister Bruno Le Maire scrolled through the official White House notification on his tablet. "According to this document, our tariff rate was calculated based on 'excessive use of silent letters,' 'unnecessary cheese variety,' and 'historical rudeness to American tourists asking for ketchup.'"

Meanwhile in Washington, Trump was holding court in the Rose Garden, aggressively gesturing at a chart showing French products with their new tariffs. The chart appeared to be hand-drawn on the back of a McDonald's placemat.

"The French have been very nasty on trade, very nasty," Trump declared, attempting to pronounce 'croissant' as 'KWAH-sont.' "They send us these cheeses—hundreds of cheeses! Who needs that many? America has already perfected cheese. It comes individually wrapped in plastic and lasts forever. That's innovation!"

Vice President JD Vance nodded gravely. "Every time an American buys a beret, a coal miner in Ohio loses his job. It's basic economics."

Back in Paris, the French Resistance 2.0 was already forming. The Minister of Culture unveiled an emergency plan titled *"Opération Désagrément"* (Operation Annoyance), a multi-pronged retaliatory strategy.

"First," she declared, "we will immediately increase the snobbery coefficient of all French waiters by thirty percent. Any American attempting to order 'French fries' will be subjected to a minimum forty-five second judgmental stare."

"Second, we are reclassifying all French wines exported to America as 'Freedom Fermented Grape Juice' with labels featuring eagles wearing berets."

"Third, and most devastating: we are temporarily suspending the teaching of French kissing to American study abroad students."

The room gasped. This was no longer diplomacy. This was war.

In the charming village of Camembert, artisanal cheese makers gathered in emergency session. Master fromagier Claude Brie addressed his colleagues, all wearing black armbands over their white coats.

"For centuries, we have crafted cheeses that smell like unwashed feet because that is the smell of CULTURE," he declared, pounding his fist on a wheel of Roquefort for emphasis. "Now Trump demands we make our cheeses more 'nose-friendly' and suggests we add 'cool ranch' flavor!"

The assembled cheese masters collectively retched.

"I propose," continued Brie, "that we develop a special export cheese for America called 'Le Trump'—it will appear gold-plated on the outside but consist of hollow processed cheese product within. It will pair perfectly with self-delusion."

At Louis Vuitton headquarters, designers worked frantically to develop "tariff-proof" luxury goods. The new "MAGA Collection" featured handbags with twice as many unnecessary pockets, red white and blue leather, and a special compartment for concealed firearms. Each bag came with a certificate of authenticity still identifying it as French-made, but with a sticker declaring "ASSEMBLED WITHIN VISUAL DISTANCE OF AMERICAN SOIL" to confuse customs officials.

Macron addressed the nation in a somber televised speech, wearing a navy blue suit but with a subtle American flag handkerchief peeking from his pocket—fashion diplomacy at its finest.

"Citizens of France," he began, "for generations we have endured American mispronunciation of our language. We have watched them dip our sacred baguettes in RANCH DRESSING. But these tariffs? *C'est trop!*"

He unveiled France's official response: a reciprocal 20% tariff on American cultural exports, primarily affecting superhero movies, tweets written in all-caps, and anything labeled "world champion" for competitions only Americans play.

The French Parliament approved an additional measure requiring all American tourists to pass a basic test on European history before being allowed to say "back-to-back World War champs."

In a final act of devastating cultural retaliation, France announced it would begin referring to Trump's signature hair style as "*le poulet frit*" – fried chicken.

Trump, upon hearing this news while examining gold-plated bathroom fixtures, immediately announced plans to increase the tariff to 25%, citing "hair-based aggression."

He then leaned close to the mirror and whispered to his reflection: "They're just jealous of our freedom fries."

Chapter 3
Italy: La Dolce Tariffa

Prime Minister Giorgia Meloni was in the middle of her morning espresso ritual—the sacred fifteen seconds of silence Italians observe before the first sip—when her phone erupted with a notification tone that sounded suspiciously like someone breaking spaghetti in half.

Her face contorted into an expression of horror typically reserved for tourists asking for pineapple pizza. The message read: "BREAKING: TRUMP IMPOSES 18% TARIFF ON ITALIAN

GOODS, CITES 'EXCESSIVE HAND GESTURES DURING TRADE NEGOTIATIONS' AS JUSTIFICATION."

"Mamma mia!" she exclaimed, her espresso cup clattering dramatically to the floor in slow motion. "This is an act of economic terrorism! Call an emergency cabinet meeting! And someone bring more coffee—this requires at least three more espressos to process!"

Within the hour, the Italian cabinet assembled in Rome, everyone talking simultaneously and gesticulating so vigorously that the chandelier swayed. Finance Minister Giancarlo Giorgetti attempted to explain the American rationale while reading from the official White House statement, his free hand performing gymnastics of outrage.

"IMPOSSIBLE!" he shouted, thrusting the document overhead like a soccer referee issuing a red card. "According to this CRIMINALLY INSANE document, our tariff was calculated using a formula that combines the average arm movement during trade negotiations, multiplied by the number of syllables Italians add to English words, divided by how many times Americans mispronounce 'bruschetta'!" He paused to kiss his fingertips in reverse—the Italian gesture for catastrophic disgust. "They also claim our pasta has an 'aerodynamic advantage' over American pasta because it 'twirls more efficiently'!"

In Washington, Trump stood in the White House briefing room beside a large poster showing Italian products with red X's over them. The chart was titled "MAKING AMERICAN FOOD GREAT AGAIN" with a subtitle in smaller letters: "By Eliminating Competition From Foods People Actually Enjoy."

"Italy has been very, very mean to us on pasta," Trump declared, mispronouncing "pasta" as "PASS-ta." "They've been making pasta for thousands of years – thousands! – while we've been making the best pasta for maybe fifty years. It's not fair. We need time to catch up!"

Vice President JD Vance nodded solemnly. "Every time an American consumes authentic Italian olive oil, a patriotic American soybean weeps petroleum tears of abandonment. These tariffs aren't just about economics—they're about preventing our domestic vegetable oils from developing crippling inferiority complexes. Studies show that exposure to real Parmigiano-Reggiano can cause American cheese singles to experience existential crises and spontaneously melt in shame."

In Parma, the headquarters of Italy's prosciutto consortium had transformed into a war room. Chairman Antonio Falcone addressed his fellow producers, who had all draped their butcher coats with funeral-black sashes bearing the words "*MAI GROSSO*" – "Never Thick."

"Trump claims our prosciutto is 'too thinly sliced' and gives us an 'unfair deliciousness advantage' over American ham!" Falcone thundered, waving the tariff notification so vigorously it created a small breeze. "He demands we make our prosciutto 'thicker, less flavorful, and more American-friendly'!"

"SACRILEGE!" cried the assembled producers, crossing themselves reflexively.

"I will slice my own finger before I slice prosciutto as thick as American deli meat!" declared one elderly producer, dramatically drawing his slicing knife for emphasis.

In Naples, the situation was even more volatile. The Association of Neapolitan Pizzaioli called an emergency demonstration in which ten thousand pizza makers simultaneously threw their arms up and exclaimed "*MA CHE CAZZO!*"—an expression of disbelief so powerful it registered on local seismographs.

Master pizzaiolo Salvatore Esposito addressed the crowd: "Trump has specifically targeted Neapolitan pizza because it makes American chain pizza look like cardboard with ketchup! He suggests we add hot dogs in the crust to receive a tariff exemption!"

The crowd responded with a collective gesture so obscene it could be seen from space.

Italy's diplomatic response was swift and passionate. Foreign Minister Antonio Tajani delivered a blistering seventeen-minute rebuke in which his hands never stopped moving, sometimes forming shapes not previously known to human anatomy. The speech required three translators working in shifts, one of whom fainted from gesture-related exhaustion.

The Italian Parliament unanimously approved "Operation Vendetta Culinaria," a multi-pronged response:

1. Immediate 100% tariff on American "Italian-style" products, especially targeting anything labeled "I Can't Believe It's Not Italian!"

2. Revocation of "Italian Cuisine Rights" for any American establishment using garlic bread, fettuccine Alfredo, or chicken parmesan – "none of which are actual Italian foods!"

3. Deployment of "Nonna Special Forces" – a crack team of Italian grandmothers dispatched to infiltrate American kitchens and slap wrists when pasta is overcooked.

4. Mandatory emotional support groups for Italian exporters forced to witness Americans breaking spaghetti before cooking or—horror of horrors—cutting it with a knife.

In the picturesque village of San Gimignano, renowned for its towers and olive oil production, farmer Giuseppe Vincenti stood in his ancestral olive grove, visibly distressed.

"Trump says our olive oil has 'too much flavor complexity' com-pared to American vegetable oil!" he lamented to the CNN camera crew. "He suggests we 'dumb it down' by adding artificial butter flavor! My trees have been producing oil since before America existed!"

To demonstrate his outrage, Vincenti performed the Italian "confrontation escalation sequence"—a series of increasingly elab-orate hand gestures culminating in the double-handed "what is wrong with your brain" temple rotation.

Meloni's televised address to the nation became an instant classic of Italian political oratory. Speaking from a podium festooned with basil, tomatoes, and mozzarella arranged in the Italian flag pattern, she alternated between passionate declarations of cultural pride and devastating culinary insults.

"Trump would put ketchup on his mother's funeral pasta!" she proclaimed in the speech's most quoted line, performing the Italian "chef's kiss of disgust"—similar to a regular chef's kiss but followed by mock spitting.

As the crisis intensified, Italian intelligence intercepted White House communications revealing Trump's ultimate demand: Italy must acknowledge American pizza as "superior" to receive tariff exemptions.

The Italian response was a single text message from Meloni to the White House containing only the words "*PIZZAIOLO VAF-FANCULO*" repeated seventeen times, which diplomatic transla-tors politely rendered as "We respectfully decline to compromise our culinary integrity."

Chapter 4

The Great Digital Escape

Celebration at the World Stupid Cat Video Association

The mood at the emergency meeting of the World Stupid Cat Video Association (WSCVA) in Bucharest was unlike anything in the organization's storied 11-year history. While trade organizations worldwide were drowning in despair over Trump's tariffs, the WSCVA headquarters—a converted internet café with questionable WiFi—was erupting in celebration.

"UNTARIFFABLE!" shouted Председатель Alexandru Popescu, the group's Romanian-Russian founder and self-proclaimed "Chief Feline Content Officer," as he popped a bottle of sparkling wine that was definitely not champagne. "Trump cannot tariff the digital realm! Our stupid cat videos shall flow freely across borders, untouchable by his tiny hands!"

The assembled content creators—an international coalition of people who had found their calling in filming cats being spectacularly unimpressive—cheered wildly. An Estonian woman famous for her "Cat Fails to Jump Compilation Vol. 37" series sprayed everyone with the not-champagne.

"For years, people have mocked us," continued Popescu, his accent thickening with emotion. "They said, 'Get real job!' They said, 'Stop filming cat trying to fit in too-small box!' But who is laughing now? Not the German luxury car manufacturers! Not the French wine exporters! Only us... and our cats... who are laughing because we put cucumber behind them when they were not looking!"

The WSCVA's Chief Economist (a title bestowed upon whoever had taken at least one economics class) explained the situation for those present: "Physical goods crossing borders get hit with tariffs. But our cat videos? They zoom through undersea cables and satellite transmissions, invisible to customs agents! Trump can't put a border checkpoint on the internet!"

A PowerPoint slide appeared showing projections of "Estimated Growth in Cat Content Market Share Post-Tariff Implementation," featuring a line graph that had clearly been drawn freehand with a mouse.

"Our Russian colleague's video 'Mr. Whiskers Sits on Keyboard During Important Zoom' used to compete with Italian luxury handbags for American consumer dollars," the economist explained. "Now handbags cost 18% more, but Mr. Whiskers costs the same! Economic advantage: cats!"

The association's sudden prominence had not gone unnoticed. Representatives from major industries had begun reaching out about potential partnerships.

"The Swiss watchmakers want to know if we can hide watch advertisements inside our cat videos," announced the Director of Strategic Alliances (previously the coffee delivery person). "The Japanese electronics manufacturers are asking if cats can demonstrate their products without triggering tariffs. Even the French perfume industry wants to explore if smell can be digitized and delivered via cat video!"

As the celebration reached its peak, the association's IT person (the only one who actually knew how to upload videos properly) rushed in with breaking news.

"Trump just tweeted!" he announced breathlessly. "He says he's heard about a 'very suspicious cat video loophole' and is instructing the 'cyber department' to look into 'digital tariff technology' immediately!"

A brief hush fell over the room before Popescu dismissed the threat with a wave of his hand.

"Impossible! Even Trump cannot tariff packets of data. By the time they figure out how to try, we'll have evolved to quantum cat videos transmitted directly into people's brains!"

The celebration resumed with renewed vigor as someone played their most popular video: a compilation of cats knocking items off shelves, now rebranded as "Cats Destroying Tariffable Physical Goods: An Economic Statement."

In the corner, a marketing executive frantically drafted a new slogan: "WSCVA: When Everything Else Costs More, Stupid Cats Stay Free."

As the night wore on, a toast was raised to an unlikely hero: a president who, in his quest to tax everything that moved across a border, had inadvertently made stupid cat videos the world's most economically competitive content.

The digital economy had found its moment, one hairball at a time.

Chapter 5

Moldova: Grape Expectations

President Maia Sandu of Moldova was enjoying her morning
ritual—reviewing economic indicators while sipping coffee from

her "World's 4th Poorest Country in Europe" mug—when her foreign minister burst into her office, face pale as chalk.

"Madam President! Trump has imposed a 31% tariff on all Moldovan exports to the United States!"

Sandu lowered her coffee slowly. "Is this some kind of joke? We barely export anything to America."

"It's no joke. The White House announcement just came through," the minister replied, handing her a tablet. "According to this, our tariff was calculated based on 'excessive post-Soviet vibes,' 'strategic wine advantage,' and 'being suspiciously hard to find on a map.'"

Sandu stared at the document in disbelief. "There must be some mistake. Most Americans don't even know Moldova exists. We're the country people confuse with Moldavia, which doesn't even exist anymore."

In the White House Situation Room, Trump was pointing at a world map where Moldova had been circled in red marker, with "???" written beside it.

"Moldova has been taking advantage of us for years," Trump announced to his bewildered economic advisors. "Tremendous advantage. They make wine—very good wine, people say. I don't drink wine myself, but people tell me it's excellent—and they sell it for much less than American wine because they use foreign grapes. Very unfair to American grapes!"

Commerce Secretary Lutnick cleared his throat nervously. "Sir, our annual imports from Moldova total approximately $24 million, primarily in the form of wine, apparel, and some machinery."

"TWENTY-FOUR MILLION!" Trump exclaimed, slamming his fist on the table. "That's almost twenty-five million! Highway robbery! How many Americans even know where Mol...Maldo...this place is? Very suspicious country. Probably made up."

Vice President JD Vance nodded soberly. "Many hardworking Americans in Ohio haven't even heard of Moldova, yet they're forced to compete with Moldovan... whatever it is Moldova makes. This is exactly the kind of globalist conspiracy undermining American greatness."

Back in Chişinău, Moldova's tiny capital city, an emergency cabinet meeting had been convened in what was formerly a high school gymnasium.

"Our total exports to America are smaller than what a single Walmart in Texas makes in a day," explained Economy Minister Dumitru Alaiba, gesturing to a PowerPoint slide showing Moldova's modest trade figures. "We export less to America than the average Instagram influencer makes in sponsored posts about teeth whitening."

Foreign Minister Mihai Popşoi adjusted his glasses. "According to our intelligence, Trump believes Moldova is either part of Russia or 'that place where vampires come from,' which is actually Romania. He has also referred to us three times as 'Moldor,' which I believe is from Lord of the Rings."

President Sandu massaged her temples. "So we've been hit with a tariff by a country whose president doesn't know we exist, targeting exports we barely send there, calculated using a methodology that involves our location being 'suspiciously Eastern European'?"

"Precisely, Madam President," nodded the finance minister. "Trump has also specifically mentioned our wine exports as a national security threat because—and I'm quoting directly—'wine makes people too relaxed to fight wars properly.'"

In the vineyards of Mileştii Mici, home to the world's largest wine collection, master vintner Ion Druţă was explaining the tariff situation to his bewildered colleagues.

"Trump believes our underground wine cellars, which contain over two million bottles, are actually missile silos pointed at America," Druță sighed, gesturing around the 200-kilometer network of underground tunnels filled with wine barrels. "He thinks we're using 'wine technology' to undermine American grape farmers."

One elderly winemaker crossed himself. "But America is over 9,000 kilometers away! Our missiles—if we had any, which we don't—couldn't possibly reach that far."

"Trump believes Moldova is located 'somewhere near New Jersey,'" Druță replied wearily. "His geographic knowledge is... limited."

The Moldovan government, operating on a national budget smaller than the endowment of a mid-sized American university, struggled to formulate a response. Their three-person trade delegation (which doubled as the national badminton team) was dispatched to Washington with what resources they could muster.

Upon arrival at the State Department, the delegation was initially mistaken for lost tourists. When they finally secured a meeting with a mid-level trade official, things didn't improve.

"I understand you're from...Molvania?" the official said, squinting at his notes.

"Moldova," corrected delegation leader Natalia Gavrilița. "We're here about the 31% tariff."

"Right, Moldovia," the official nodded, mispronouncing it again. "The President has identified your country as a key threat to American economic interests due to your overwhelming wine supremacy."

"Our total wine exports to America are less than what the Trump Winery produces in a month," Gavrilița explained patiently. "In fact, our entire GDP is smaller than the net worth of the average American billionaire."

The official consulted his notes again. "According to this, President Trump believes Moldova is using—and I quote—'Soviet-era mind control techniques to make American consumers crave Eastern European wine instead of beautiful American wine from places like my fantastic vineyard in Virginia.'"

When the Moldovan delegation requested a meeting with higher-level officials, they were told that the Secretary of Commerce was busy "learning to pronounce Moldova correctly" and would be available "once he masters the syllables."

In a desperate move, the Moldovan government sent Trump a gift basket containing their finest wines, a map clearly showing Moldova's location, and a children's book titled "M is for Moldova: Yes, We're a Real Country."

The White House acknowledged receipt with a thank you note addressed to "The Republic of Moldavia" with a handwritten postscript from Trump: "Never heard of you, but your wine is FANTASTIC. Best wine from Middle-earth I've ever tasted!"

As implementation day approached, Moldova's president addressed the nation in a televised speech that was periodically interrupted by power outages.

"My fellow Moldovans, America has imposed a tariff on our exports because their president thinks we're either fictional, vampires, or Russians. While this is obviously absurd, I'm afraid there's little we can do about it. Our entire military consists of 6,000 soldiers and one helicopter that only flies if it's not too windy."

She continued with a sigh, "Therefore, we will redirect our wine exports to European markets, where people can at least locate us on a map. And we'll survive this the same way we've survived everything else in our complicated history—by being so small and poor that eventually everyone forgets about us again."

In a final twist of irony, on the day the tariffs were implemented, U.S. Customs officials discovered they had no existing import code for Moldova in their systems. After several hours of confusion, they created a new category under "Fictional Countries/Middle-earth," listing the tariff as "31% plus whatever Hobbits normally pay."

Chapter 6
Finland: The Silent Treatment

Prime Minister Petteri Orpo was enjoying a traditional Finnish breakfast of coffee, more coffee, and contemplative silence when his phone vibrated with news of Trump's tariffs. He glanced at the notification, revealing that Finland had been hit with a 15% tariff on all exports.

He blinked once.

This was the Finnish equivalent of total emotional meltdown.

After a full seven minutes of uninterrupted silence, Orpo finally spoke. "Hmm," he said, setting a new national record for verbose overreaction.

The emergency cabinet meeting that followed was characterized by what foreign observers might mistake for a group meditation session. Fourteen ministers sat around a table, stoically staring at a PowerPoint slide displaying the tariff rates. No one spoke for twenty-three minutes. Two ministers nodded slightly. Finance Minister Riikka Purra took a sip of coffee.

The tension was unbearable.

Finally, Foreign Minister Elina Valtonen broke the silence. "Trump says our tariff rate was calculated based on 'excessive national happiness rankings,' 'unfair sauna advantage,' and 'suspicious winter survival skills.'"

The room erupted in chaos—three people simultaneously raised an eyebrow.

Meanwhile in Washington, Trump was explaining his Finnish tariff policy while attempting to locate Finland on a map of Europe, his finger hovering somewhere over Portugal.

"Finland has been very unfair to us on... uh... trees and fish and those little phones they used to make. Very unfair! They sit up there with all that snow, acting all quiet and superior with their free healthcare and education. It's psychological trade warfare!"

Vice President JD Vance nodded sagely. "The average Finnish baby receives 5,376 more hours of parental leave than an American baby. This creates an unfair developmental advantage that ultimately leads to adults capable of reading, understanding science, and feeling secure in life. How can American workers compete with that?"

In Helsinki, the Finnish Sauna Association convened an emergency sweat session. Twenty elderly men sat naked on wooden benches, occasionally throwing water on hot stones, saying absolutely nothing. This was indistinguishable from their regular Tuesday meeting, except for the slightly more aggressive water-throwing, which experts recognized as the Finnish equivalent of mass hysteria.

The American embassy in Helsinki reported "unusual activity" when a crowd of approximately thirty Finns gathered outside, standing six feet apart from each other due to cultural preference for personal space, silently holding signs that read "We Respectfully Disagree" and "This Is Somewhat Disappointing."

No chanting occurred. One person briefly considered sighing loudly but thought better of it.

Finland's official response came in the form of a government press release consisting of a single page with the words: "We notice your tariffs. We will adjust accordingly."

International analysts described it as "the most passive-aggressive diplomatic communication since Norway's famously understated objection to Soviet airspace violations during the Cold War, which consisted entirely of the phrase 'We observed your aircraft.'"

Finnish paper industry executives met in an emergency sauna summit to discuss the impact on their exports. CEO Matti Virtanen of UPM-Kymmene addressed his colleagues while periodically throwing water on the sauna stones: "Trump claims Finnish paper gives Americans 'excessive paper cuts' due to its superior quality."

His colleagues nodded grimly, their stoic expressions unchanged despite the 100°C temperature. One executive permitted himself to mutter "*perkele*" under his breath—the Finnish equivalent of a nuclear verbal assault.

In the northern province of Lapland, reindeer herders received news of a specific 22% tariff on reindeer products with typical Finnish pragmatism.

"The reindeer do not care about tariffs," observed herder Aslak Näkkäläjärvi, gazing stoically across the tundra. "The reindeer care about lichen and not being eaten by wolves. Perhaps Americans could learn from the reindeer."

When asked by CNN what countermeasures Finland might take, Näkkäläjärvi stared silently at the reporter for forty-seven seconds before responding: "When you live through Finnish winter, you learn there are worse things than tariffs. Americans think 15% is a crisis. We call it Tuesday."

The Finnish Meteorological Institute announced it would suspend exports of "Finnish winter expertise" to the United States, a move experts calculated would extend American winter by approximately 17 minutes annually.

In a particularly devastating blow, Finland threatened to withhold its yearly contribution to the Strategic Nordic Happiness Reserve, which could lower global contentment levels by as much as 0.4% according to the UN World Happiness Report.

Finland's most aggressive response came from Minister of Transportation Kaisa Juuso, who announced that Finland would no longer share its winter road maintenance technology with America. "Let them figure out how to drive on ice themselves," she said, in what Finns recognized as an unprecedented display of hostility equivalent to a declaration of war in most other countries.

Prime Minister Orpo finally addressed the nation in a televised speech lasting a record-breaking three minutes and twenty-two seconds. He stood at a podium, silent for the first minute, occasionally sipping water.

"Americans think our silence means we have nothing to say," he finally stated. "In reality, we have nothing to say to foolishness."

He then revealed Finland's ultimate countermeasure: a comprehensive program to export even higher quality paper, more innovative technology, better education outcomes, and increased national happiness—all while maintaining a facial expression that could be mistaken for mild constipation.

"We will respond to these tariffs by continuing to be increasingly, unbearably competent," Orpo concluded. "Eventually, they will understand that this is the Finnish way of saying *'hyvää päivää ja haista vittu.'*"

The press release accompanying the speech helpfully translated this as "Good day and please reconsider your position."

Finnish linguists noted this was not an entirely accurate translation.

Chapter 7

United Kingdom: Keep Calm And Tariff On

Prime Minister Keir Starmer was enjoying his morning cup of Earl Grey and reviewing the latest polling numbers—a ritual that normally brought him a moment of serenity before the inevitable chaos of British politics descended—when his phone pinged with an urgent message from Downing Street's diplomatic office.

"Bloody hell," he muttered, tea sloshing dangerously close to his pristine white shirt cuff. "Trump's done what?"

The message was clear and alarming: President Trump had imposed a 17% tariff on all British exports to the United States, claiming the UK had an "unfair historical advantage" and "suspicious linguistic superiority."

"Get me Foreign Secretary Lammy immediately," Starmer barked at his assistant. "And someone ring the Palace. His Majesty needs to be informed."

In the White House Rose Garden, Trump was addressing the press while pointing at a large poster board featuring the Union Jack with a red "X" through it.

"The United Kingdom—which, by the way, isn't even that united, lots of people are saying this—has been taking advantage of America for decades," Trump declared. "They send us their fancy accents, their royal dramas on Netflix, and their snooty TV cooking judges, and what do we get? Nothing but cars with the steering wheel on the wrong side!"

Vice President JD Vance nodded gravely. "Hard-working Americans shouldn't have to compete with people who sound like they're smarter just because they pronounce 'schedule' as 'shed-yule.' It's linguistic elitism, plain and simple."

When a reporter from the Washington Post pointed out that Britain had been America's closest ally for over a century, Trump scoffed.

"They burned down the White House, you know. Very few people know this. Terrible allies. And they still have a king! A king! Very medieval. Very unfair to American presidents who have to leave after eight years."

At Buckingham Palace, King Charles III was in the royal gardens, earnestly explaining sustainable farming practices to his beloved plants when his private secretary approached with the news.

"A tariff? On British goods?" Charles set down his pruning shears, his expression darkening. "On what grounds?"

The secretary cleared his throat uncomfortably. "According to the White House statement, sir, the tariff was calculated based on 'excessive royal family drama advantage,' 'unfair tea-drinking superiority,' and 'colonial-era grudges.'"

The King's face went through several remarkable contortions as he attempted to maintain royal composure. "I see," he said finally, in the tone of a man who absolutely did not see at all. "And has the Prime Minister formulated a response?"

"There's an emergency COBRA meeting in an hour, Your Majesty. But..." the secretary hesitated.

"Out with it, man," urged the King.

"President Trump has specifically requested your personal intervention. He claims—and I quote directly, sir—'King Charles and I have a special relationship. Great guy. Very king-like. He's going to call me, and we'll work this out king-to-president, monarch-to-monarch.'"

Charles' eyebrows ascended to previously unknown heights. "He does realize I'm a constitutional monarch, not an absolute one?"

"The White House seems unclear on this distinction, sir."

In the Cabinet Office Briefing Room A (COBRA), the British government's emergency response team had assembled. Foreign Secretary David Lammy was attempting to explain Trump's specific grievances.

"According to our embassy in Washington, Trump believes the BBC gives us 'unfair cultural influence.' He specifically mentioned 'Downtown Abbey' as anti-American propaganda designed to make Americans feel inferior about their lack of butlers."

"Downton Abbey," corrected the Culture Secretary automatically.

"Yes, well, he called it 'Downtown,' and he believes it's a documentary," Lammy sighed. "He also claims British accents give us an 'unfair negotiating advantage' because Americans 'think anyone who sounds like James Bond must be telling the truth.'"

Chancellor of the Exchequer Rachel Reeves looked grim as she examined the economic projections. "The impact could be severe. The U.S. is our largest single export market. This would affect everything from Scotch whisky to Burberry coats."

"What about our special relationship?" asked the Defense Secretary. "Two hundred years of alliance thrown away because Trump thinks Downton Abbey is real?"

"He also mentioned something about us having too many queens," added Lammy uncomfortably. "Both the royal kind and. .. well, he made some rather undiplomatic comments about British pop culture."

Prime Minister Starmer pinched the bridge of his nose. "Right. We need a multi-pronged approach. Diplomatic channels, economic negotiations, and..." he hesitated, looking pained, "I believe we may need to deploy His Majesty."

At this, the room fell silent. The nuclear option.

Later that afternoon, in a heavily fortified chamber beneath Buckingham Palace that hadn't been used since the Cold War, King Charles sat before a secure video link, receiving an emergency briefing from Britain's top diplomats and cultural experts.

"Your Majesty, our relationship with President Trump is... complicated," explained the chief diplomat delicately. "He has a peculiar fascination with monarchy and seems to believe you have powers similar to those of Henry VIII."

"Whom he likely believes is still alive," muttered a cultural attaché under her breath.

"We've prepared some talking points," continued the diplomat, sliding over a folder. "But most importantly, sire, we need you to... well..."

"Charm him," finished the Prime Minister bluntly. "God help us all."

Charles flipped through the briefing folder with increasing alarm. "It says here he thinks London Bridge is actually falling down? And that I personally control the weather over Scotland?"

"Yes, sir. He also believes you have the ability to grant him a genuine lordship, not just one of those novelty titles tourists buy online."

The King closed the folder with a sigh that carried the weight of a thousand years of monarchy. "The things one does for one's country."

The video call with Trump was scheduled for the following morning. The White House insisted it be conducted with "full royal regalia" because, as Trump's Chief of Staff explained, "The President expects to see a real king, not just some old guy in a suit."

Reluctantly, Charles appeared in his full coronation finery, complete with the Imperial State Crown and scepter, despite pointing out repeatedly that monarchs didn't typically conduct diplomacy while looking "like the Monopoly man at a costume party."

The call began with Trump immediately launching into a monologue about his own "royal-like qualities."

"You know, King Charles—can I call you King? Great name, by the way, very kingly—many people say I would have made a tremendous king. The best king. My hotels are basically castles. Gold everywhere. Very royal."

Charles, with the patience developed through seven decades of waiting for the throne, nodded politely. "Indeed, Mr. President. Now, regarding these tariffs—"

"The tariffs, yes, beautiful tariffs," Trump interrupted. "Did you know the UK sends us shortbread cookies but calls them 'biscuits'? Very confusing for American shoppers. And your cars have the steering wheel on the wrong side. Completely backward! Not to mention all those British actors taking Hollywood jobs from hard-working American actors."

"Mr. President," Charles tried again, "the United Kingdom and the United States have enjoyed a special relationship for—"

"Special, yes, very special. Like me and Melania. Beautiful woman, Melania. Speaking of beautiful women, how's that daughter-in-law of yours? The American one? Fantastic addition to your royal family. Made it much better, if you ask me. Much more watchable."

Charles gripped his scepter so tightly his knuckles turned white. "Mr. President, perhaps we could discuss a resolution to these tariffs that would benefit both our nations?"

Trump leaned forward conspiratorially. "Here's the deal, King—and I make the best deals, everyone says so—I'll drop the tariffs completely if you do three simple things. First, knight me. Sir Donald sounds fantastic, doesn't it? Second, admit that American tea is better than British tea. And third, give us back that giant diamond in your crown. We've got the perfect spot for it in the Trump Tower lobby."

The Imperial State Crown suddenly felt very heavy indeed.

Outside 10 Downing Street, the British press had assembled, sensing disaster. The BBC's political correspondent cornered the Cabinet Secretary as he rushed in with armfuls of crisis documents.

"Is it true," she asked, "that President Trump has demanded knighthood in exchange for tariff relief?"

"No comment," the secretary replied, in a tone that clearly meant "dear God, yes."

Across Britain, industries braced for impact. In Scotland, whisky distillers gathered in emergency sessions, facing the horrifying prospect of a 17% price increase on their American exports. "Two hundred years of distilling tradition threatened because Trump thinks Braveheart was a documentary," lamented the head of the Scotch Whisky Association.

In the Midlands, luxury automakers faced an existential crisis. At the Aston Martin factory, executives watched in horror as their stock price plummeted.

"Trump specifically mentioned us," said the CEO, reading from the White House statement. "He claims our cars have an 'unfair James Bond advantage' and give British motorists 'excessive coolness not available to Chevrolet drivers.'"

As panic spread, British creativity flourished. The Foreign Office launched "Operation Flattery," a multi-platform campaign highlighting Trump's "kinglike qualities" across British media. The BBC hastily commissioned a documentary titled "Trump Towers: America's Castles," while British newspapers published suspiciously positive editorials about Trump's "regal bearing" and "hands of unmistakably royal proportion."

In a particularly desperate move, Madame Tussauds unveiled a new Trump wax figure, inexplicably dressed in royal regalia with a plaque reading "Perhaps The Greatest King Britain Never Had."

After a week of intensive negotiations, the Palace announced a compromise: King Charles would bestow upon Trump the ceremonial title "Honorary Lord Protector of Anglo-American Trade Relations"—a completely invented position with a sufficiently grand-sounding name and an impressively large but utterly meaningless certificate.

In return, Trump agreed to reduce the tariff from 17% to 15%, which he announced as "the greatest trade deal in the history of trade deals, maybe ever" despite it being essentially the same tariff with a trivial reduction.

In his public address following the agreement, Prime Minister Starmer embodied the great British tradition of making catastrophic defeat sound like dignified compromise:

"Today, we have reached an understanding with our American allies that reflects the deep, abiding special relationship between our nations. While challenges remain, this agreement demonstrates that diplomacy, patience, and the judicious deployment of monarchy can still achieve marginal improvements in dire situations."

Behind closed doors, however, he was overheard telling his staff: "Next time, we're sending the bloody corgis to negotiate. They couldn't possibly do worse."

At Buckingham Palace, King Charles returned to his garden, speaking even more intensely to his plants.

"At least you," he told a particularly sympathetic rose bush, "understand the true meaning of dignity."

Chapter 8
Scotland: Och Aye The No

First Minister John Swinney was enjoying a dram of Islay single malt in his Edinburgh office when his phone buzzed with the news: Trump had imposed a 17% tariff on UK goods, with an additional 4.5% "regional specificity tariff" on Scottish exports.

"Awa' an bile yer heid!" Swinney exclaimed, whisky spilling on his desk. "A twenty-one-point-five percent tariff on Scotland? Whit's the clarty dobber thinkin'?"

His advisor handed him the official White House statement. According to the document, Scotland's additional tariff had been calculated based on "excessive bagpipe advantages," "unfair whisky-making head starts," and "the incomprehensible accent bonus that confuses American negotiators."

In an emergency session of the Scottish Parliament, SNP, Labour, and even Conservative MSPs united in unprecedented harmony to denounce the tariffs.

"Trump claims our accent gives us an 'unfair trade advantage' because American negotiators cannae understand when we're insulting them," explained Finance Secretary Shona Robison, her Glasgow accent thickening with indignation. "Apparently, we've been bamboozlin' them for years by soundin' like we're speakin' English when we're actually speakin' 'Scottish.'"

"Does he think we're speakin' in code?" asked one bewildered MSP.

"Aye, essentially," Robison nodded. "His exact words were: 'The Scots say things like "Haud yer wheesht" and "Ye wee scunner" while smiling, and our negotiators think they're being complimented.'"

In Speyside, the heart of Scotland's whisky country, distillery owners gathered in emergency session at The Craigellachie Hotel. Master distiller Moira MacPherson of Glenfiddich addressed her colleagues, her face flushed with righteous anger.

"Trump claims our whisky has an 'unfair maturation advantage' because—and I quote directly—'Scotland was making whisky while America was still being discovered, very unfair head start, the most unfair.'"

"The bampot doesnae even drink alcohol!" shouted another distiller. "He thinks whisky is made from potatoes!"

"Worse," replied MacPherson grimly. "He suggested we could resolve the tariff by adding 'beautiful American ingredients like high-fructose corn syrup' to make our whisky 'less intimidating to Americans who prefer sweeter drinks.'"

The assembled distillers erupted in outrage so intense it was barely comprehensible even to other Scots.

In the Highlands, Scotland's bagpipe manufacturers faced their own crisis. At MacGregor & Sons, crafters of fine bagpipes since 1742, old Duncan MacGregor read the tariff notification with disbelief.

"It says here our pipes have a 'tactical acoustic advantage' that gives Scotland 'unfair cultural penetration into American parades,'" he growled, his Highland accent so thick it seemed to physically thicken the air. "Trump thinks we're usin' the pipes as some kind of sonic trade weapon!"

His son Hamish checked the White House statement on his phone. "He's suggested we could avoid the tariff by developing 'quieter, more American-friendly bagpipes' or adding a mute button."

"A MUTE BUTTON?" The elder MacGregor's face turned the color of a well-cooked haggis. "The man's a total rocket! Next he'll want us tae add Bluetooth and auto-tune!"

Scotland's textile industry wasn't spared either. In the Borders region, tartan weavers received news that their products faced tariffs because they contributed to "unfair Scottish identity advantage" and "excessive cultural distinction in formal wear."

"Trump thinks we invented tartan just last week to confuse the American fashion industry," explained textile union representative Fiona McTavish, her Borders accent rolling like the hills around her. "He believes we're 'hiding secret messages in the patterns' to give Scottish negotiators an edge."

First Minister Swinney, recognizing the gravity of the situation, attempted to reach Trump directly. After seventeen transferred calls and being placed on hold while "Scotland the Brave" played mockingly through the White House phone system, he finally got through to a senior advisor.

"Could you please explain to the President," Swinney began with forced patience, "that the Scots language and our accent are not negotiating tactics?"

"I'm sorry," replied the advisor, "but the President is convinced your incomprehensible speech patterns are an 'acoustic tariff' on American ears. He's suggested you could reach a compromise by 'speaking American' in all future trade discussions."

"Ye mean ENGLISH?" Swinney exploded, his accent thickening with every word. "The language we bloody invented?!"

"Sir, I can't understand what you're saying right now, which just proves the President's point."

As Scotland faced economic catastrophe, centuries of battling against seemingly insurmountable odds kicked in. Throughout history, Scotland had survived English invasion, Highland Clearances, and the Scottish national football team's World Cup performances. They would survive Donald Trump.

The Scottish government launched "Operation Braveheart," a two-pronged strategy: publicly complying with America's demands while secretly redirecting exports through English ports with fake "Made in Generic Britain" labels.

Additionally, distilleries began producing special "Trump-Friendly" whisky—regular whisky in bottles adorned with golden thistles and labels proclaiming it "EXTREMELY SMOOTH AND TREMENDOUS, NOT SCARY AT ALL."

In Glasgow, shipbuilders unveiled plans for what they claimed was a "revolutionary American-inspired vessel" but was actually a standard ship with an enormous gold "T" painted on the hull.

Scottish Twitter—a legendary force in global social media—mobilized with ruthless efficiency. Within hours, #TrumpCantScareAScot and #TariffsArePish were trending worldwide, accompanied by memes so linguistically impenetrable that Trump's social media team couldn't determine if they were being complimented or savagely insulted. (They were being savagely insulted.)

When Trump tweeted that Scottish people should "speak more American and less gibberish," Edinburgh University's linguistics department responded with a comprehensive 18-thread explanation of how English evolved from Scots-Anglo Saxon, ending with the succinct: "We're nae speakin' gibberish, ye absolute roaster, ye're jist thick as mince."

As implementation day approached, First Minister Swinney addressed his nation from the steps of the Scottish Parliament:

"For seven hundred years, Scotland has faced down those who would diminish our culture, silence our voices, or water down our whisky. Today we face a man who wants to do all three, but cannae even find us on a map without confusing us with Ireland.

"We survived Edward Longshanks, we survived the Highland Clearances, and we'll survive this absolute bawbag of a president and his tariffs. Scotland wasn't built on backing down—we were built on standing up, speaking our minds, and making whisky strong enough to put hair on your chest and fire in your belly.

"So let Trump have his tariffs. When the dust settles, we'll still be here, still incomprehensible, still making the world's finest whisky, and still playing bagpipes at a volume that makes ears bleed. Because that's what it means to be Scottish!"

As the speech went viral globally, Trump tweeted: "Scottish PM making nice comments about me and my tremendous tariffs! Very respectful! I've always loved the Scotch people, my mother was one!"

In whisky distilleries across Scotland, master distillers quietly added another cask to the "Special Reserve"—whisky being aged specifically until Trump leaves office, at which point it will be bottled under the name "The Last Laugh."

The label, printed but kept in storage, features a cartoon of Trump being chased by a haggis wearing a kilt, with the tagline: "Worth the wait, ye glaikit numpty."

Chapter 9
Theater Review: "Tariff On The Roof"

By Jonathon Mercer, Chief Theater Critic, The New York Times
Richard Rodgers Theatre, Broadway

In what must surely qualify as the most improbable Broadway hit since "Hamilton" reimagined the Founding Fathers with hip-hop, "Tariff on the Roof" opened last night to thunderous applause from an audience that included three former Treasury

Secretaries and Martha Stewart (who, in a delightful coincidence, sells a kitchenware line made in seven countries currently under tariff).

Adapting Trump's global trade wars into a musical comedy is either an act of theatrical genius or utter madness. Director Marvin Moskowitz, fresh from his Tony for "Impeach Pit" (the surprisingly heartwarming musical about the Senate cafeteria workers during political crises), has somehow managed to transform dry economic policy into a showstopper that had audience members simultaneously laughing, crying, and checking their investment portfolios.

The show opens spectacularly with "If I Were A Rich Country," performed by Anthony Azizi as a beleaguered Chinese trade minister, standing atop a rotating set of shipping containers while customs agents dance with increasingly large calculators. The number ends with the now-iconic moment where calculators explode in puffs of smoke as the tariff percentages exceed their computational capacity.

Aaron Tveit brings surprising depth to the role of Trump, avoiding easy caricature in favor of a complex portrayal of a man who genuinely believes Liechtenstein is "hiding something" and that Belgian waffles are made by "waffle-hoarding Europeans with suspicious grid technology." His second-act solo, "Tariffs Are The Prettiest Sound," performed while lovingly polishing a gold-plated calculator, brought an unexpected poignancy to what could have been mere satire.

The breakout star, however, is clearly Viola Davis as the increasingly desperate Director of Customs and Border Protection. Her show-stopping number "Calculate!"—performed while frantically trying to apply seventeen different tariff rates to a single Italian sports car—is an extraordinary feat of vocal dexterity. Davis somehow manages to sing entire verses while appearing to have an authentic nervous breakdown, culminating in her climbing atop the car and declaring, "Fine! It's 400% on everything! Math is for globalists!"

The supporting cast shines in the international ensemble numbers. Particularly memorable is "Matchmaker, Matchmaker, Find Me An Export," performed by a chorus of increasingly desperate Canadian diplomats attempting to explain that they're actually part of North America. The choreography here is inspired, with the Canadians performing increasingly strenuous politeness rituals that go completely unnoticed by Tveit's Trump, who is busy autographing pictures of Vermont.

Not all numbers land as successfully. "Do You Hear The Nations Sing?", featuring representatives from 193 UN member states trying to explain basic geography to Trump, runs a bit long at seventeen minutes, though the visual spectacle of the rotating globe set with increasingly confused lighting cues saves it from tedium.

The second act cleverly structures itself around the "Twelve Days of Tariffs" motif, with each day revealing a new unintended consequence. By the time we reach "twelve systems crashing, eleven budgets bursting, ten prices soaring," the audience is both laughing and wincing in recognition.

The decision to stage the "Sunrise, Sunset" homage ("Tariffs Rise, Markets Fall") as a split-stage showing simultaneous economic collapse in thirty different stock exchanges is technically ambitious. The moment when all thirty traders collapse in synchronized heart attacks while Trump tweets "WINNING!" may be the darkest joke ever to receive a standing ovation on Broadway.

The production design deserves special mention. The White House set transforms seamlessly from the Oval Office to the Situation Room to Mar-a-Lago, often mid-song, while projected tweets appear and disappear with nightmarish rapidity. The costume de-

sign for the "Dancing Dollars" chorus, with their sequined currency symbols that transform from euros to yuan to pesos with each
spin, will surely earn Tony consideration.

If the show has a flaw, it's in occasionally trying to explain actual economics. A mid-second-act number featuring Janet Yellen
(a wonderfully dry Allison Janney) attempting to explain tariff
incidence theory through interpretive dance drags slightly, though
it picks up when she's joined by a chorus of economists whose increasingly frantic movements culminate in them forming a human
graph that collapses.

The finale, "To Life (Tariffs For Everyone)," performed by
the entire international cast wearing price tags that increase in
real-time via digital costume technology, brings the show to a rous-
ing conclusion. As Trump stands atop a golden desk signing executive orders that drop as confetti while the global economy literally
burns around him (impressive pyrotechnics here), one can't help
but marvel at how something so economically devastating has been
transformed into such joyous entertainment.

In the show's most quoted line, Tveit's Trump gazes out at a
world he's economically shattered and declares with genuine puz-
zlement, "If everyone's paying tariffs, shouldn't America be rich by
now?" The audience's laughter was tinged with enough genuine
anxiety to suggest that "Tariff on the Roof" isn't just brilliant
theater—it's necessary catharsis.

Four stars out of four. Expect a long run and higher ticket prices.
Ironically, not subject to tariff.

Chapter 10
Russia: The Tariff That Wasn't

In the gilded halls of the Kremlin, where opulence attempted to mask the increasingly desperate state of the Russian economy, President Vladimir Putin sat in stony silence as his Foreign Minister delivered the unexpected news.

"Mr. President," Sergei Lavrov began cautiously, "it appears that when Trump announced his global tariffs, Russia was... omitted from the list."

Putin's face remained as expressionless as it had been since his last Botox appointment, though a tiny vein pulsing in his temple suggested that somewhere beneath the carefully cultivated exterior, actual human emotions might exist.

"Omitted?" Putin replied, his voice carrying the warmth of a Siberian winter. "Trump has instituted tariffs against virtually every nation on Earth, including uninhabited Antarctic islands, and he simply... forgot Russia?"

Prime Minister Dmitry Medvedev, seated nearby and attempting to appear relevant, cleared his throat. "Not exactly forgotten, Vladimir Vladimirovich. The White House statement specifically mentions that Russia is exempt from the tariff program due to, and I quote, 'special relationship considerations.'"

Putin's eyes narrowed to dangerous slits. After decades of cultivating an image as the world's premier geopolitical villain, being publicly identified as America's "special friend" was possibly the most devastating blow to Russian prestige since the fall of the Soviet Union.

"This is catastrophic," Putin said quietly, rising to stare out the window at Moscow, where ordinary Russians were struggling with an economy shattered by sanctions, military failures, and the third consecutive year of what state media had optimistically dubbed "temporary wartime challenges."

"I was counting on those tariffs," he continued, addressing his reflection in the window rather than his increasingly nervous advisors. "Do you understand what American tariffs would have meant for us?"

Lavrov and Medvedev exchanged confused glances.

"Higher prices on exports?" ventured Medvedev hesitantly. "Reduced trade volume? Economic hardship?"

Putin spun around, a rare animation crossing his features. "Exactly! Glorious, American-imposed economic hardship! The perfect scapegoat!"

He began pacing, the most physical activity his security detail had witnessed in months.

"For two years, I have promised the Russian people that victory in Ukraine was just around the corner. For two years, I have asked them to endure empty shelves, worthless rubles, and mobile crematoriums returning their sons. Their patience is running thin."

Putin's voice dropped to a conspiratorial whisper. "We needed those tariffs. We needed to tell our people that their suffering was caused by America, not by the special military operation that was supposed to be over in three days."

At the state-run Channel One television studio, news producers were frantically revising that evening's propaganda broadcast. The original script, prepared in anticipation of Trump's tariffs, had featured the headline "AMERICA DECLARES ECONOMIC WAR ON RUSSIA" alongside footage of triumphant Russian soldiers and weeping Ukrainian civilians that had been repurposed from a Romanian soap opera.

"What are we supposed to lead with now?" demanded the network's director. "We've spent two years blaming everything on American aggression, and now Trump has specifically NOT attacked us? How do we spin this as Western hostility?"

In Moscow's Red Square, where a small crowd had gathered in anticipation of the tariff announcement, confusion reigned. The pre-printed signs reading "DOWN WITH AMERICAN ECONOMIC IMPERIALISM" seemed suddenly irrelevant.

"So America is... not targeting us?" asked a bewildered pensioner. "But state television said American tariffs were going to be the reason my pension buys less bread this month."

A nearby FSB agent quickly escorted him away for "routine questioning about bread expectations."

Back in the Kremlin, Putin had retreated to his private office to make a very unusual phone call. After multiple security protocols and scrambling measures, the call connected to Mar-a-Lago.

"Donald, it's Vladimir," Putin began, his voice uncharacteristically emotional. "What is the meaning of this tariff exemption?"

Trump's voice boomed through the secure line. "Vlad! Great to hear from you, buddy. Great job on the exemption, right? I took care of you, just like we discussed. No tariffs for Russia! You're welcome!"

"That's precisely the problem," Putin hissed. "I never asked to be exempted. Quite the opposite. I NEEDED those tariffs!"

A confused silence followed.

"You... wanted me to impose tariffs on Russia?" Trump finally asked.

"Of course! My economy is collapsing, my people are restless, and the war is a disaster. I needed an external enemy to blame! What am I supposed to tell Russians now? That their suffering is because of MY decisions?"

Trump's response was typically self-centered. "So you're saying you WANT tariffs? I could add them. I could add them right now! Best tariffs you've ever seen. Huge tariffs. Special tariffs just for Russia."

"No, it's too late," Putin sighed. "The damage is done. You've publicly called Russia your 'special friend.' Do you have any idea what that does to my carefully cultivated image as the world's most frightening leader?"

As he hung up, Putin stared blankly at the portrait of Peter the Great on his wall. "Perhaps," he mused to himself, "we could pretend the tariffs exist anyway? After all, if state media says American

tariffs are destroying the economy, who would know the difference?"

That evening, Russian television nonetheless announced that
"Cruel American tariffs have been imposed on Russian goods,"
while showing footage of empty grocery shelves that had actually
been empty since 2022.

Sometimes in Russia, the most useful economic policies were
the ones that didn't actually exist.

Chapter 11
Canada: Classified Canadian Diplomatic Cables

CABLE #1
FROM: Canadian Embassy, Washington D.C.
TO: Prime Minister's Office, Ottawa
CLASSIFICATION: CONFIDENTIAL
SUBJECT: Initial Response to Trump Tariff Announcement

Prime Minister Carney,

I regret to inform you that President Trump has announced a 25% tariff on Canadian lumber, automobiles, and "anything else that seems too Canadian." The announcement came during what was supposed to be a routine call about cross-border fishing rights but quickly devolved into a 17-minute monologue about how maple syrup is "suspiciously sticky" and gives Canada an "unfair pancake advantage."

When I attempted to explain the integrated nature of our economies, the President interrupted to ask if Ryan Reynolds could be reclassified as an American export since "he's in too many of our movies" and that "Deadpool is definitely American, not Canadian, because he has guns and makes inappropriate jokes." I did not have the heart to explain that Deadpool's irreverent humor and tendency to apologize after violence is quintessentially Canadian.

Official diplomatic response has been drafted along standard Canadian protocol lines (Expression of Disappointment Level 3: "Deeply Concerned But Still Polite").

With sincere regret,
Ambassador Wilson

P.S. Please note that President Trump still believes you are related to Mariah Carey. All attempts at correction have failed.

CABLE #2
FROM: Ministry of Finance, Ottawa
TO: All Canadian Diplomatic Missions
CLASSIFICATION: INTERNAL ONLY

SUBJECT: Actual Economic Impact Assessment (DO NOT SHARE WITH AMERICANS)

Team,

While our public economic analysis suggests "moderate concern," actual projections indicate what internally we're classifying as a "complete and utter hoser situation."

Our economists have calculated that explaining basic trade economics to the Trump administration would require approximately 147,000 PowerPoint slides, 328 puppets, and a hockey-based analogy so simplistic it would be insulting to children.

For public consumption, please continue using our approved talking points about "mutual prosperity" and "integrated supply chains." For internal planning, please implement Emergency Protocol: "Sorry Not Sorry"—which, for our newer staff members, is our strategic response plan where we publicly apologize while simultaneously implementing targeted countermeasures. (Remember: we say "sorry" while applying the economic equivalent of a body check into the boards.)

Also, please note that Minister Freeland broke her "swear jar" after reading the tariff list. A replacement is being ordered.

With maple-flavored despair,
Deputy Minister Johnson

CABLE #3
FROM: Canadian Border Services Agency
TO: Prime Minister's Office
CLASSIFICATION: SECRET
SUBJECT: Operation Passive Resistance

PM Carney,

As requested, we have begun implementing Phase 1 of "Operation Passive Resistance." Border agents have been instructed to be "aggressively Canadian" toward American visitors, including:

1. Increasing instances of saying "sorry" by 200%, but with 50% less sincerity

2. Asking detailed questions about American visitors' hockey knowledge

3. Temperature control "malfunction" at all border stations (setting: "Winnipeg in February")

4. Playing Nickelback on continuous loop in all customs areas

5. Replacing Fox News with CBC documentaries about sustainable forestry practices in all waiting areas

Early results show a 78% increase in American visitors questioning their life choices.

Standing on guard,
Commissioner Bouchard

CABLE #4
FROM: Canadian Embassy, Washington D.C.
TO: All Government Ministries
CLASSIFICATION: TOP SECRET

SUBJECT: Counterintelligence Report: Trump's Tariff Calculation Method Discovered

After extensive investigation, we have identified the formula used by the Trump administration to calculate Canada's tariff rates:

(Number of times Trump has been told poutine isn't American × Canadian Olympic hockey gold medals ÷ America's perceived politeness deficit + number of times Justin Trudeau's hair has been mentioned on Fox News) × random number Trump saw on a gas station sign

This formula was discovered on a McDonald's napkin in the Oval Office, alongside a crude drawing of a moose wearing a tuque labeled "enemy of American freedom."

Please adjust economic models accordingly.

In bewildered service,
Intelligence Division

CABLE #5
FROM: Prime Minister Mark Carney
TO: Cabinet and Senior Staff
CLASSIFICATION: EYES ONLY
SUBJECT: The Gloves Are Coming Off (Politely)

Team,

While I maintained diplomatic composure during my press conference, please be advised that behind closed doors I used language that would make a hockey player blush. The transcript has been sealed and will only be released when we need to scare future generations of politicians.

I have just concluded a call with President Trump during which he suggested we "just become part of America" as a solution to the tariff issue. When I declined, he asked if we could "at least send over Shania Twain as a gesture of goodwill."

Implement Countermeasure Package C, which we will publicly refer to as "Proportional Economic Response" but which we all know is Operation "Sorry About Your Luck."

Also, effective immediately, all government communications should replace "America" with "Our Friends To The South" using the most passive-aggressive tone possible.

Retain our dignity at all costs. Remember: we're playing the long game here. Winter is coming, and we've had more practice.

Politely but firmly,
Mark

P.S. I've approved the strategic maple syrup reserve release. God help us all.

CABLE #6
FROM: Canadian Tourism Board
TO: Prime Minister's Office
CLASSIFICATION: CONFIDENTIAL
SUBJECT: Emergency Tourism Campaign

PM Carney,

As directed, we have prepared an emergency tourism campaign specifically targeting Americans who are "disappointed with recent trade policies." The campaign slogan "Canada: Like America, But With Healthcare And Without The Tariffs" has tested extraordinarily well with focus groups.

Television advertisements will feature Ryan Gosling explaining universal healthcare while chopping wood, followed by a moose wandering through an affordable pharmacy. The closing shot shows a real American family calculating how much they would save on insulin by simply moving 20 miles north.

We've also secured Drake for a new national anthem remix that subtly highlights the economic benefits of an integrated North American economy while remaining "unforgettably catchy."

Budget requires approval by Friday.

Patriotically yours,
Director Williams

P.S. Céline Dion has volunteered to perform directly outside Mar-a-Lago every morning at 5 AM until tariffs are lifted. Awaiting your authorization.

CABLE #7
FROM: Canadian Embassy, Washington D.C.
TO: Prime Minister's Office
CLASSIFICATION: URGENT**SUBJECT:** Unexpected Development

Prime Minister,

During what was supposed to be a routine briefing, Vice President Vance asked me if Canada and North Dakota were "basically the same place" and whether we could "just merge them and call it a day."

When I attempted to explain the concept of national sovereignty, he showed me a map where he had colored Canada as "North

North Dakota" and asked if we'd be willing to "just go with it" in exchange for a tariff exemption.

Before I could respond, he suggested that if we weren't amenable to the North Dakota proposal, perhaps we would consider becoming "America's Hat" officially, with a special ceremony where you would be presented with a pin in the shape of America that you would wear "like a brooch."

Please advise on appropriate response that maintains diplomatic relations while preserving our dignity as a sovereign nation.

Awaiting instructions with what remains of my patience,

Ambassador Wilson

FINAL CABLE
FROM: Prime Minister Mark Carney
TO: ALL CANADIANS
CLASSIFICATION: PUBLIC RELEASE
SUBJECT: A Message to All Canadians About Our Response to U.S. Tariffs

My fellow Canadians,

Today I addressed the nation regarding President Trump's tariffs on Canadian goods. As you know, publicly I expressed "deep concern" and called for "renewed dialogue."

What you did not see was that immediately after the cameras stopped rolling, I skated onto the frozen Rideau Canal, performed a perfect hockey stop that sprayed ice in the exact shape of a middle finger, and screamed into the cold void of winter for approximately seven minutes.

Let history record that in Canada's darkest hour, we responded as true Canadians: we were unfailingly polite to their faces while passive-aggressively judging everything about them behind their backs.

Remember, fellow Canadians: we survived prohibition, we survived the disco era, and we've survived every winter since confederation. We will survive Donald Trump.

The true north strong and free,
Mark Carney, Prime Minister

P.S. If anyone asks, this message never existed. Sorry about that.

Chapter 12
Puerto Rico: Tariffing Ourselves

Governor Pedro Pierluisi of Puerto Rico was enjoying his morning café con leche when his Chief of Staff burst into his office, face drained of color.

"Governor, President Trump just announced a 23% tariff on all Puerto Rican exports to the United States."

Pierluisi choked mid-sip. "That's impossible. We're part of the United States. You can't tariff yourself."

His Chief of Staff handed him a tablet displaying the official White House press release. There it was in black and white: a 23%

tariff on Puerto Rico for "unfair Caribbean trade advantages and suspicious use of two official languages."

"There must be some misunderstanding," Pierluisi muttered. "Get me the White House on the phone."

Three hours and seventeen phone transfers later, Pierluisi finally reached Commerce Secretary Howard Lutnick.

"Mr. Secretary, there's been a grave error. Puerto Rico is a U.S. territory. We're American citizens. The President cannot impose tariffs on domestic trade."

A long pause followed. "Hold please," Lutnick said.

Pierluisi was treated to five minutes of "The Star-Spangled Banner" played on what sounded like a kazoo before Lutnick returned.

"Governor, I've consulted with the President, and he says—and I'm quoting directly—'If they're Americans, why do they speak Mexican?'"

"We speak Spanish and English, and neither language determines our citizenship status," Pierluisi explained, massaging his temples. "Could I speak with the President directly?"

"He's currently busy drawing new tariff numbers on a map of places he doesn't recognize. Can I take a message?"

The following day, Pierluisi flew to Washington for an emergency meeting. After waiting six hours in the White House lobby, he was finally ushered into the Oval Office, where Trump was putting golf balls into a coffee mug.

"Mr. President, thank you for meeting with me. I'm here about the tariffs on Puerto Rico."

Trump looked up. "Puerto Rico! Beautiful country. Beautiful beaches. I almost built a golf course there once. Would have been the best golf course in the entire foreign country of Puerto Rico."

"Sir, that's precisely the issue. Puerto Rico is not a foreign country. We're a U.S. territory. Puerto Ricans are American citizens. We have been since 1917."

Trump squinted suspiciously. "If you're American, why is your island floating in the ocean away from America?"

"Hawaii is also—" Pierluisi began, then thought better of it. "Sir, geographically, we're in the Caribbean, but legally and politically, we're part of the United States. We use the U.S. dollar. We serve in the U.S. military."

"So you're saying you have soldiers? Is that a threat?" Trump's eyes narrowed further.

"No, sir, I'm saying Puerto Ricans serve in the United States military—your military. Over 200,000 Puerto Ricans have served in the U.S. armed forces."

Trump nodded thoughtfully, then said, "But you don't vote for president."

"That's correct, we cannot vote in presidential elections despite being citizens, which is a separate issue we could discuss—"

"AHA!" Trump exclaimed, pointing a triumphant finger. "Non-voters! Very suspicious. Only Americans vote. That's how you know they're American."

"But we are Americans who legally cannot vote for president because of our territorial status."

"Sounds like something a foreign country would say to avoid tariffs," Trump replied, returning to his putting.

The meeting continued for another forty-five minutes, during which Pierluisi presented historical documents, legal precedents, and even pulled up the U.S. government's own websites confirming Puerto Rico's status, all to no avail.

When Pierluisi mentioned that Puerto Rico uses U.S. postal services, Trump became excited.

"The Post Office? I love the Post Office. Great American institution. Are you saying you stole our Post Office? Very illegal. Very bad. We might need to increase the tariff for Post Office theft."

Back in Puerto Rico, Pierluisi convened an emergency cabinet meeting.

"It's hopeless," he announced. "I spent an hour explaining our relationship to the United States, and he ended the meeting by offering to sell Puerto Rico back to ourselves at 'a very special price, the best price.'"

Secretary of State Elmer Román looked grim. "I tried reaching Vice President Vance. He suggested we could solve the problem by officially changing our name to 'South Florida' and 'acting more American,' whatever that means."

Treasury Secretary Juan Zaragoza shook his head. "I spoke with Commerce Secretary Lutnick again. When I explained that imposing tariffs on Puerto Rico would be like the U.S. imposing tariffs on itself, he said, and I quote: 'The President sees this as an absolute win-win.'"

A week later, Pierluisi made one final attempt, arranging a video call with Trump that included several prominent Puerto Rican veterans in full U.S. military uniform.

"Mr. President, these distinguished Puerto Ricans have all served in the United States military, defending American freedom and values. They are American citizens."

Trump studied the screen. "First, thank you for your service to whatever country you're from. Second, if you're American soldiers, why are you calling from overseas? Very suspicious."

"Sir, we're not overseas in the military sense. Puerto Rico is American soil."

"Then why do I need to call you on a special video call thing? I don't need a special call to talk to Ohio."

"Because you invited us to this call, sir."

Trump nodded sagely. "Exactly my point."

As implementation day approached, a desperate Pierluisi made one last attempt, sending Trump a gift basket containing American flags, a bound copy of the Jones–Shafroth Act of 1917 (which granted Puerto Ricans U.S. citizenship), and a note reading: "FROM YOUR FELLOW AMERICANS IN PUERTO RICO."

The White House acknowledged receipt with a formal thank you letter addressed to "The Foreign Nation of Puerto Rico" with a handwritten note from Trump: "Thanks for the flags! Very nice of you to celebrate America despite being so foreign."

On April 9th, as the tariffs took effect, U.S. Customs and Border Protection agents arrived at San Juan's ports looking profoundly confused.

"So we're supposed to collect tariffs on goods... that are already in the United States... to be shipped to... the United States?" one agent asked his supervisor.

"Don't ask questions," the supervisor replied. "Just collect 23% of something from somebody."

When Puerto Rican businesses began receiving their first tariff bills—effectively paying the U.S. government for the privilege of engaging in domestic commerce—Governor Pierluisi delivered a resigned address to his constituents:

"My fellow Americans—because that's what we are, regardless of what President Trump believes—I have exhausted every possible avenue to educate the President about our status. I have presented historical documents, legal precedents, military records, and even a children's book titled 'P is for Puerto Rico: Part of the USA.'

"The President responded by suggesting we take a 'very good, very fair citizenship test' to prove we're Americans. When I reminded him that Puerto Ricans are already citizens by birth, he said that sounded like something non-citizens would say to avoid taking a test.

"Therefore, I am announcing the formation of a new government department: the Ministry of Explaining Basic Geography

and Political Status to Dense Presidents. The department's first action will be implementing our new strategy: waiting for someone
else to be elected."

As American citizens prepared to pay tariffs to their own government for goods that never cross an international border, a
White House staffer was overheard asking, "Sir, if Puerto Rico is
foreign, why do they use the U.S. dollar?"

Trump's response perfectly encapsulated the situation: "Another excellent point. They're counterfeiting our currency too! Increase the tariff to 25%!"

Chapter 13

Operation Waffle Iron

The Great Belgian Breakfast Raid

At precisely 7:32 AM Eastern Time, as Americans across the country were settling into vinyl booths for their morning breakfast, Operation Waffle Iron commenced. Three thousand Customs and Border Protection agents simultaneously entered 1,948

Waffle House locations across 25 states, their windbreakers embla-
zoned with the hastily created "Breakfast Border Patrol" insignia.

The mission: locate and collect tariffs on all Belgian waffles being
consumed on American soil.

At the Waffle House on Interstate 85 outside Atlanta, Special
Agent Derek Chambers adjusted his tactical sunglasses and surveyed the crowded restaurant. His team had been briefed at 4 AM
with a PowerPoint presentation titled "Waffle Identification and
Tariff Implementation Protocols," which primarily consisted of
pictures of various breakfast foods with the words "AMERICAN"
or "FOREIGN" stamped across them.

"Remember your training," Chambers muttered to his
three-agent team. "Belgian waffles have deeper grid patterns than
American waffles. They're taller. More... Belgian."

The agents nodded solemnly and fanned out through the
restaurant, clipboards at the ready, peering intensely at customers'
plates.

At booth seven, Agent Chambers spotted his first target: a retired couple sharing a large Belgian waffle topped with strawberries
and whipped cream.

"Customs and Border Protection," he announced, flashing his
badge. "I need to see some documentation for that waffle."

The couple stared in bewilderment.

"Documentation?" the husband finally managed.

"Import papers. Certificate of waffle origin. Proof of tariff payment," Chambers clarified, pulling out his official CBP calculator.
"I'm afraid that appears to be a Belgian waffle, which is now subject
to the President's 22% Breakfast Tariff Initiative."

"But... we ordered it from the menu. Right here," the wife
protested, pointing at the laminated menu.

Chambers shook his head grimly. "The menu clearly states 'Belgian Waffle.' Foreign designation. That'll be $1.76 in tariffs, please."

Across the restaurant, Agent Melissa Rodriguez had cornered a bleary-eyed truck driver whose plate contained the remnants of a Belgian waffle.

"Sir, I'll need you to step away from the syrup," she instructed. "That waffle has not cleared customs."

"It's just called a Belgian waffle!" the trucker protested. "It's made right here in the kitchen! By Chuck!" He pointed to the grill cook, who waved spatula in confirmation.

Rodriguez consulted her manual. "Sir, according to Tariff Implementation Directive 7B, any waffle marketed or presented as 'Belgian' falls under the President's executive order regardless of actual production location. The designation creates an 'unfair breakfast prestige advantage' over American-style waffles."

Meanwhile, at the counter, Agent Tyler Johnson was explaining to a confused waitress that the restaurant would now need to implement a two-tier waffle payment system.

"Customers can pay for the waffle itself as normal," he explained, "but the 22% tariff must be collected separately and placed in these official Treasury Department Waffle Revenue bags." He held up a ziplock bag with "WAFFLE TARIFF" written on it in Sharpie.

"But our Belgian waffles are made with the same batter as our regular waffles," the waitress protested. "We just use a different iron to make the squares bigger."

Johnson's eyes narrowed. "Are you admitting to waffle nationality fraud? That's a federal offense under the new regulations."

At a Waffle House in Chattanooga, a college student attempted to outsmart the system by ordering "a waffle of unspecified national origin with extra-deep grid patterns." The local CBP agent was having none of it.

"Nice try, son. If it looks Belgian, sits Belgian, and syrup-pools Belgian, it's Belgian. That'll be $2.13."

At a Charlotte location, agents discovered a customer attempting to disguise his Belgian waffle as American by cutting off the edges to make it appear smaller. He was issued a warning for "waffle tampering with intent to evade tariffs."

The chaotic breakfast raids continued throughout the morning. In Houston, a six-year-old girl burst into tears when agents confiscated her Mickey Mouse-shaped Belgian waffle because her parents couldn't pay the tariff. The agents eventually accepted payment in quarters from her Frozen piggy bank, issuing a handwritten receipt on a napkin.

By 10 AM, the operation had hit a snag. The special tariff collection app developed overnight by a Treasury Department intern had crashed nationwide, forcing agents to calculate rates by hand. Making matters worse, their government-issued calculators had run out of battery because, as one supervisor explained, "They're from China, and the replacement batteries are stuck in customs due to the electronics tariff."

Meanwhile at CBP headquarters, Commissioner Rodriguez was on a video call with a very angry Secretary of Commerce Howard Lutnick.

"You deployed three thousand agents to Waffle Houses?" Lutnick was shouting. "We meant for you to check for Belgian waffle imports at PORTS OF ENTRY! The commercial shipments of frozen waffles from actual Belgium!"

"But the directive specifically said to enforce tariffs on 'all Belgian waffle consumption on American soil,'" Rodriguez protested, reading from the memo. "It says nothing about ports or imports."

"BECAUSE THAT'S WHAT CBP ALWAYS DOES!" Lutnick roared. "We didn't think we needed to specify that we didn't want you harassing IHOP customers at breakfast!"

As the fallout spread, White House Press Secretary Karoline Leavitt clarified the administration's position: "President Trump's Belgian Waffle Tariff is meant to protect American breakfast sovereignty. For too long, foreign breakfast concepts have dominated our morning meals, putting undue pressure on pancakes, which, as you know, are the President's preferred breakfast food."

By noon, Operation Waffle Iron was officially suspended. Agents were recalled from Waffle Houses nationwide, leaving behind confused customers, traumatized waitstaff, and approximately $43,850 in collected tariffs (mostly in loose change and crumpled dollar bills stuffed into ziplock bags).

The following morning, Waffle Houses across America debuted a new menu item: "Freedom Waffles—100% American, Definitely Not Belgian, No Tariff Required."

In a final twist, a subsequent Treasury Department audit revealed that the entire Belgian waffle tariff effort had cost approximately $2.7 million to implement, making it possibly the least cost-effective tariff in American history.

President Trump, however, declared it a tremendous success, tweeting: "American breakfast is SAFE AGAIN! Belgium waffle monopoly BROKEN! Pancakes RISING to record levels! #BreakfastBorders #MakeMorningsGreatAgain"

Copyright and Disclaimer

Oops. I almost forgot this.

IMPORTANT SATIRICAL DISCLAIMER
This is a work of satire. Names, characters, businesses, places, events, locales, and incidents are either the products of the author's imagination or used in a fictitious manner. Any resemblance to actual persons, living or dead, or actual events is purely coincidental, except for Donald Trump, who unfortunately exists.

No actual tariffs were harmed in the making of this book.

The author and publisher are not responsible for any diplomatic incidents, trade wars, or economic collapses that may result from taking this book seriously. The U.S. Customs and Border Protection agents depicted raiding Waffle Houses are fictional, and readers should not attempt to pay tariffs on their Belgian waffles.

If you're a government official looking to implement any of the policies satirized herein, please seek immediate professional help.

LEGAL NOTICE REGARDING TARIFFS

The author of this work makes no claims to expertise in international trade policy, economics, or arithmetic—much like the administration depicted within these pages.

Readers experiencing symptoms of uncontrollable laughter, sudden bursts of economic clarity, or the urge to check if uninhabited Antarctic islands are actually subject to tariffs should be advised that these are normal reactions to absurdity.

****

First Edition: April 2025
ISBN: 979-8-9922852-6-0
Library of Congress Control Number: no idea
Cover design by Barry Robbins
Printed in the United States of America on paper that may or may not be subject to tariffs, depending on the current presidential mood.

Chapter 14

Jamaica: Special Report

CNN's Jamaica Tariff Investigation

CNN correspondent Brianna Matthews adjusted her blazer in the sweltering Kingston heat as the camera operator counted down. "Three, two, one..."

"I'm Brianna Matthews reporting live from Kingston, Jamaica, where President Trump's sweeping new 22% tariff on Jamaican exports has locals concerned about economic impacts. We're here to get perspectives from everyday Jamaicans about these controversial trade policies."

The carefully planned segment was part of CNN's "Global Voices on American Tariffs" series, which had already featured bewildered Swiss bankers, outraged German autoworkers, and a particularly memorable French cheese maker who had expressed his feelings by silently staring into the camera while dramatically cutting a wheel of Camembert for ninety uncomfortable seconds.

Matthews had spent three hours with her producer searching for the perfect interview subject—someone authentic, articulate, and visually representative of Jamaica. When they spotted Desmond Johnson lounging beside his roadside fruit stand, wearing a knitted red, gold, green, and black tam hat over his dreadlocks and casually enjoying what was definitely not a cigarette, the producer had whispered excitedly, "That's our guy! Perfect optics!"

Matthews approached with her most professional smile. "Excuse me, sir? I'm with CNN. We're doing a story about President Trump's new tariffs on Jamaican exports. Would you be willing to share your thoughts?"

Desmond regarded her through a haze of fragrant smoke, his eyes narrowing thoughtfully before breaking into a wide grin. "Ya wan' talk 'bout Trump tax? I man can explain de whole situation, star. Camera ready?"

The producer gave an enthusiastic thumbs-up, envisioning the perfect clip of authentic Jamaican outrage for the evening broadcast. Matthews positioned herself next to Desmond and nodded to the camera operator.

"I'm here with local businessman Desmond Johnson. Mr. Johnson, how do you feel about the 22% tariff President Trump has imposed on Jamaican exports?"

Desmond took a long, contemplative drag before exhaling thoughtfully. "Ya see, sista, de whole ting is a manifestation of

Babylon system, ya understand? Trump—him a Babylon incarnate. Him tariff is just modern colonialism, seen?"

Matthews nodded encouragingly, mentally calculating how much of this would need to be subtitled.

"De 22% number not accidental," Desmond continued, warming to his subject. "Twenty-two divide by two is eleven. Eleven plus eleven is twenty-two. Double numbers represent duality. Trump creating duality between nations instead of unity. Pure Babylon mathematics."

The producer's smile froze slightly as he realized this wasn't going to be the simple "tariffs hurt our economy" soundbite he'd hoped for.

Matthews tried to redirect. "How specifically will these tariffs affect Jamaica's economy?"

"Economy?" Desmond laughed, a deep, melodious sound. "What is economy but a construct of Western oppression? Jamaica no need economy. We have sun, earth, water, and herb." He gestured to his modest fruit stand. "I grow food, I eat food, I sell food. No tariff can tax de sun, ya understand?"

"But surely Jamaica's exports—coffee, rum, bauxite—will be affected by these tariffs?" Matthews pressed.

"Listen now," Desmond leaned closer, his voice dropping conspiratorially. "Trump put tariff on tings, but him can't put tariff on consciousness. Jamaica export music, culture, spiritual vibration. How him gonna tax Bob Marley? How him gonna tariff reggae rhythm? Impossible!"

The producer was frantically making cutting motions, but Matthews was genuinely intrigued. "That's an interesting perspective. So you're saying Jamaica's most valuable exports are cultural and therefore tariff-proof?"

"Exactly, sista!" Desmond beamed, impressed by her quick understanding. "De most valuable tings can't be taxed. Love, music, wisdom—dem cross borders like wind. Trump building walls but can't stop de breeze."

He paused to take another thoughtful puff. "And consider dis: Jamaica import American culture for decades—Hollywood, hip-hop, fast food. Where our tariff? We should charge America 22% cultural influence tax, seen? Balance de scales!"

Matthews found herself nodding along, captivated by his alternative economic theory despite her producer's increasingly desperate signals.

"Final question, Mr. Johnson. What message would you send to President Trump about these tariffs?"

Desmond pondered for a moment, then broke into a radiant smile. "Tell Trump come Jamaica. Sit on beach. Smoke herb. Listen reggae. In one week, him forget all 'bout tariff and start movement for global unity, star!"

"You think smoking marijuana would change Trump's trade policies?" Matthews asked, unable to hide her amusement.

"One love solve everything," Desmond said with absolute conviction. "Even Trump heart can open with right herbal meditation."

As the camera stopped rolling, the producer approached, looking distressed. "That was... not what we expected. I'm not sure we can use any of that."

But Matthews was scrolling through her phone, where notifications were already flooding in. The interview, streaming live on CNN's social media, was going viral. #TariffTheBreeze was trending, and economic professors from Harvard to Oxford were earnestly debating whether cultural exports should indeed be considered in trade balance calculations.

Meanwhile, Desmond had returned to his fruit stand, completely unfazed by his sudden international fame. When Matthews thanked him for the interview, he simply smiled and handed her a perfectly ripe mango.

"No tariff on dis one," he winked. "Sweetness is always free trade."

Chapter 15
Mexico: Nightmare On Pennsylvania Avenue

President Trump pushed away his dinner plate with a satisfied grunt, having demolished what his personal chef optimistically called "Presidential Mexican Fusion"—essentially a Trump Tower Taco Bowl with extra cheese and significantly less Mexican influence than the name suggested.

"Great food. The best Mexican food," Trump announced to no one in particular as he dabbed his mouth with a monogrammed napkin. "Much better when it's made in America. No need for their imports."

That evening, as the White House settled into its nighttime routine, Trump retired to the presidential bedroom, the lingering taste of processed cheese and store-bought salsa still on his palate. As he drifted off to sleep, a strange gurgling emanated from his midsection—the unmistakable protest of a digestive system encountering "fusion cuisine."

The nightmare began innocuously enough.

Trump found himself standing alone in the Oval Office, admiring his reflection in the window when he heard an unusual sound—like the crinkling of foil wrappers. Turning slowly, he froze in terror.

Sitting behind the Resolute Desk was an enormous taco, its hard shell gleaming menacingly under the office lights. Instead of filling, it contained stacks of tariff documents.

"We need to talk about these tariffs, pendejo," the taco said, its voice deep and gravelly.

Trump backed away, only to bump into something soft and yielding. Spinning around, he found himself face-to-face with a massive burrito, wrapped in what appeared to be pages from trade agreements.

"Thirty-eight percent? ON US?" the burrito demanded, quivering with rage and sour cream.

"I don't understand," Trump stammered. "You're food. Food doesn't talk. And food certainly doesn't question my perfect trade policies."

"We're not just food," the taco declared, slamming a lettuce-appendage onto the desk. "We're an $11 billion industry that employs thousands of workers on both sides of the border."

Trump tried to flee toward the door, but his path was blocked by a bowl of guacamole, its surface rippling ominously.

"Do you have any idea," the guacamole bubbled, "what your tariffs are doing to avocado farmers? My people are suffering!"

"Your people?" Trump squeaked. "Avocados don't have people. They're just... foreign green things."

The guacamole rose higher, forming a vaguely humanoid shape. "Seventy percent of America's avocados come from Michoacán, Mexico. That's 120,000 jobs you're threatening with your tariffs!"

Trump backed away, sweating profusely. "Jobs, shmobs. America needs to protect itself from invasive foreign... foods."

"Invasive?" The word echoed around the room as the door to the Oval Office burst open.

Floating through the doorway came a chimichanga, sizzling with righteous anger, trailing drops of hot oil that left tiny burn marks on the presidential carpet.

"We've been part of the American diet for generations!" the chimichanga boomed. "We bring people together! We create joy! And how do you repay us? Tariffs!"

Trump scrambled behind a couch. "This is ridiculous. You're not real. You're just Mexican food!"

"MEXICAN-AMERICAN food!" the assembled items corrected in unison, their voices shaking the room.

The taco leaped from behind the desk with surprising agility for a corn-based product. "We represent billions in bilateral trade! We're the foundation of countless American businesses!"

The burrito unrolled slightly, revealing economic charts where beans should be. "Your tariffs don't just hurt Mexico—they hurt American consumers who now pay more for us!"

"And American restaurants," added the chimichanga, floating menacingly closer.

"And American grocery stores," bubbled the guacamole.

"And American farmers who export corn to Mexico for our tortillas," the taco concluded.

They began to close in, surrounding Trump as he cowered behind the couch.

"What do you want from me?" he whimpered.

"We want you to understand something fundamental," the taco said, leaning in close enough that Trump could smell the cumin on its breath. "Tariffs aren't just numbers on paper. They affect real people, real businesses, real lives."

"And real food," added the burrito.

"But mostly," said the guacamole, extending a gloopy green hand toward Trump's face, "we want you to experience what it feels like to be treated as an enemy for no reason."

The chimichanga began to glow red-hot. "We want you to feel the burn of economic anxiety."

"No!" Trump cried. "No burning! I'll remove the tariffs! I'll—"

The food items exchanged glances, then turned back to Trump with what could only be described as culinary smirks.

"Too late," they said in unison. "The tariffs are already causing indigestion... in the markets."

They rushed toward him all at once—the taco crunching, the burrito unfurling, the guacamole sloshing, and the chimichanga sizzling.

Trump awoke with a gasp, bolt upright in the presidential bed, sheets soaked with sweat. Sunlight streamed through the windows as he patted himself frantically, checking for salsa stains or guacamole residue.

"Just a dream," he muttered. "Just a ridiculous dream."

But as he reached for his phone to check his morning Twitter feed, he found his hand trembling. The nightmare images remained vivid – especially the economic charts the burrito had shown him, detailing the genuine bilateral damage his tariffs would cause.

With shaking fingers, he dialed a number.

"Get me the President of Mexico," he barked at the White House operator. "Immediately."

"You mean President Claudia Sheinbaum, sir?" the operator asked.

"Yes, yes, whatever her name is," Trump snapped. "And cancel my order for taco bowls this week. Tell the chef I'm in the mood for... hamburgers. Very American hamburgers."

As he waited for the call to connect, Trump couldn't shake the feeling that somewhere, in a kitchen not far away, Mexican food was plotting its revenge.

Chapter 16
Guyana: The Forgotten Tariff

President Irfaan Ali of Guyana was enjoying his morning coffee and cassava bread when his foreign minister burst into his Georgetown office, waving a phone with such vigor that his glasses nearly flew off his face.

"Mr. President! Trump has imposed a 34% tariff on all Guyanese exports to the United States!"

Ali nearly choked on his cassava. "Thirty-four percent? Why? And why us specifically?"

The minister handed him the phone displaying the official White House announcement. According to the document, Guyana's tariff had been calculated based on "excessive natural resource advantages," "suspicious location between South America and not South America," and "unfair tropical agricultural conditions."

"This makes no sense," Ali muttered, scanning the document. "We're one of America's strongest allies in the region. Our total exports to the U.S. barely register on their economic radar."

In Washington, Trump was pointing at a large map where Guyana had been circled in red marker—though the circle actually encompassed most of Suriname and a chunk of Venezuela as well.

"Guyana has been taking advantage of us for years," Trump declared to his bewildered economic team. "Very unfair country. They have all this... stuff... that they should be sharing with America."

"What stuff specifically, sir?" ventured Commerce Secretary Lutnick.

Trump waved his hand vaguely. "You know, jungle stuff. Gold. Those little frogs that kill you if you lick them. Very valuable frogs. And they just discovered huge oil reserves! Tremendous oil. The best oil. Should be American oil."

Vice President JD Vance nodded solemnly. "The average hardworking American can't even pronounce Guyana correctly, yet they're forced to compete with their exotic exports like..." he glanced at his notes, "bauxite and sugar."

"Exactly!" Trump pointed triumphantly. "And they speak English there! Very suspicious. Why would a South American country speak English? They're clearly up to something."

Back in Georgetown, President Ali had convened an emergency cabinet meeting in the wood-paneled conference room of Guyana's modest government headquarters.

"According to our analysis," explained Finance Minister Ashni Singh, pointing to a hastily prepared PowerPoint slide, "Trump appears to believe we're hiding something from America because, and I quote directly from his tweet: 'Nobody knows anything about Guyana, which means they're very sneaky. The sneakiest!'"

Foreign Minister Hugh Todd adjusted his glasses. "Our embassy in Washington reports that when they called to discuss the tariff, the White House receptionist asked if they were calling about 'that Jonestown place where the Kool-Aid thing happened.'"

"That was 45 years ago!" exclaimed Vice President Bharrat Jagdeo, throwing his hands up in exasperation. "And it wasn't even Kool-Aid, it was Flavor Aid!"

"I'm afraid that's not our biggest problem," continued Todd. "When we finally reached someone at the Commerce Department, they admitted that Trump decided on our tariff percentage after watching a documentary about poison dart frogs. He believes we're 'weaponizing amphibians' against American interests."

The room fell silent as the cabinet tried to process this information.

"So we're being punished with a crippling tariff because we have colorful frogs?" Ali asked incredulously.

"Not just the frogs, sir," added the Agriculture Minister. "The White House statement specifically mentions our 'suspiciously large' water lily, the Victoria amazonica, calling it an 'aquatic trade advantage' that American lily pads 'cannot fairly compete with.'"

In the offices of the Guyana Rice Development Board, Executive Director Nizam Hassan was staring in disbelief at the tariff notification. Guyana's rice exports to the U.S., already modest, would now face a 34% price increase.

"Trump believes our rice has an 'unfair tropical advantage' over American rice," Hassan explained to his equally bewildered staff. "Apparently, growing rice in a tropical climate is now considered cheating in international trade."

At the Guyana Gold Board, similar scenes of confusion unfolded. Chairman Erolle Hodge gathered his team around a computer displaying Trump's latest tweet: "Guyana hiding gold from America! Very unfair! Should share with America First! Maybe we'll take it if they won't give it!"

"Is he... threatening to invade us for our gold?" asked a wide-eyed junior analyst.

"I think he's just confused," Hodge sighed. "His follow-up tweet asks why 'Guyana' and 'Ghana' sound so similar if they're not the same place, and suggests it's a 'crafty name trick' to confuse American negotiators."

As Guyana grappled with its unexpected targeting, President Ali attempted to reach Trump directly. After seventeen transferred calls and being placed on hold while "America the Beautiful" played on loop, he finally reached a White House aide.

"This is President Ali of Guyana. I urgently need to speak with President Trump about these tariffs."

"Goo-yah-nah?" the aide responded uncertainly. "Is that in Africa?"

"No, we're in South America. We've been a U.S. ally for decades. President Trump has imposed a 34% tariff on our exports and we need to understand why."

"Oh, right. The frog country. Let me see if he's available."

After another ten minutes on hold, Ali was informed that Trump was "very busy deciding on tariffs for other countries" but had left a message: "Tell Guy-anna they know what they did."

In desperation, the Guyanese government launched "Operation American Education," sending informational packets about

Guyana to the White House, Congress, and major news outlets. The packets included basic facts (location, population, main exports), a brief history explaining why an English-speaking country exists in South America, and, most critically, a note clarifying that "Jim Jones was American, not Guyanese."

They also created a simple infographic titled "Guyana vs. Ghana: Different Continents, Different Countries" after discovering that Trump had been confusing the two nations in trade meetings.

In Georgetown's small but bustling market district, ordinary Guyanese citizens were baffled by their sudden prominence in American trade policy.

"Trump thinks we're hiding gold from America?" laughed Marcus Persaud, a third-generation gold panner from the Essequibo region. "We've been trying to sell our gold to America for years! It's not hiding if you're actively trying to export it!"

At Bourda Market, rum seller Lakshmi Singh shook her head in disbelief. "How can he put tariffs on a country he couldn't find on a map? My cousin in New York says Americans think Guyana is in Africa or Asia. Some even think it's an island in the Pacific!"

As the situation deteriorated, Guyana tried one last desperate measure: they sent Trump a gift basket containing local products like Demerara sugar, El Dorado rum, and a children's book titled "G is for Guyana: Yes, We're in South America."

The White House acknowledged receipt with a thank you note addressed to "The Republic of Ghana" with a handwritten postscript from Trump: "Thanks for the rum! Fantastic rum from Africa!"

In a final bizarre twist, Trump tweeted that he would consider reducing Guyana's tariff if they agreed to "return" the Victoria amazonica water lily to the United States, apparently unaware that the lily was native to Guyana, not stolen from America.

As President Ali addressed his nation in a televised speech, he tried to maintain diplomatic composure despite the absurdity of the situation.

"My fellow Guyanese, we face an unprecedented challenge. The United States has imposed tariffs on our exports because their president appears to believe we are either hiding frogs, stealing water lilies, or possibly an entirely different country altogether.

"We have tried reason. We have tried education. We have tried diplomacy. None has succeeded. Therefore, we will do what Guyanese have always done in the face of challenges beyond our control—we will persist, we will adapt, and we will wait for more reasonable leadership to emerge.

"In the meantime, I have instructed our embassy in Washington to send President Trump a map. Not just any map, but one with very large letters spelling 'GUYANA' over our country. Sometimes the simplest solutions are the best."

The speech was met with thunderous applause across the nation, followed by the most Guyanese of responses—a collective shrug and the phrase that had sustained the small nation through countless challenges: "We gon' survive this too, man. We always do."

Chapter 17

Venezuela: Viva La Confusión

The emergency cabinet meeting in Caracas was entering its fifth hour. Venezuela's highest-ranking officials sat slumped around a massive table in the Miraflores Palace, ties loosened, jackets discarded, and expressions ranging from bewilderment to hysteria.

"Let me understand this correctly," President Nicolás Maduro said, pinching the bridge of his nose. "The United States, which already has crippling sanctions against our entire economy, has now added a specific 52% tariff on Venezuelan agricultural products because..." he squinted at the document, "because Chavez was unfair to American grape farmers?"

Foreign Minister Yván Gil nodded grimly. "And because our 'lettuce advantages' constitute an existential threat to America's salad security."

Vice President Delcy Rodríguez broke the silence. "But we barely export any agricultural products to the United States! The sanctions already prevent most trade!"

"And Chavez has been dead for ten years," added the Agriculture Minister helplessly.

"Not that Chavez," Oil Minister Pedro Tellechea clarified, scrolling through his phone. "According to Trump's latest tweets, he believes our country is run by César Chávez, the American labor rights activist who organized farm workers in California in the 1960s."

"The American? Who died in 1993?" Maduro's voice cracked with disbelief.

"The very same," Tellechea confirmed. "Trump apparently believes César Chávez is not only alive but somehow running Venezuela from beyond the grave as some kind of... agricultural revolutionary dictator."

Maduro slumped in his chair, his trademark mustache drooping with the weight of this new absurdity. Venezuela was now facing fresh economic punishment based on a three-way confusion between himself, his predecessor Hugo Chávez, and an American civil rights leader who had never set foot in Venezuela.

"Does Trump think I'm César Chávez?" Maduro asked weakly.

"No, he thinks you're Hugo Chávez," clarified the Communications Minister. "He referred to you in his press conference as 'the fat Chavez with the mustache' and asked why you changed your first name from Hugo to Nicolas but kept Chavez as your last name."

"But Chávez is not my last name! I'm Maduro! Nicolás Maduro!"

In Washington, Trump was explaining his decision to a bewildered press corps.

"Venezuela has been very nasty on lettuce," Trump declared, stabbing a finger at a chart showing agricultural imports. "Very nasty. And their leader—Hugo, César, whatever he calls himself these days—used to organize all these farm workers in California. Very unfair to American farmers!"

When a reporter pointed out that César Chávez was an American labor leader who died decades ago and had no connection to Venezuela, Trump waved dismissively.

"Fake news. Very fake. They're all connected—the Chavezes, the lettuces, the grape conspiracies. I know more about Venezuela than anyone."

Back in Venezuela, ordinary citizens adapted to this new absurdity with the weary resilience that comes from years of economic and political turmoil.

At Caracas's largest farmers' market, produce vendors had developed a brisk side business selling "Certified Non-Revolutionary" certificates to tourists.

"Want some tomatoes, mi amor?" called María Gonzalez from her produce stand. "Very fresh! Non-sanctioned! No César Chávez tax included!"

On Venezuelan television, government propaganda quickly adapted. State TV now featured hourly "educational" segments comparing images of Hugo Chávez, Nicolás Maduro, and César Chávez, explaining in excruciatingly simple terms that they were three different people, two of whom were deceased.

"For our North American viewers," intoned a serious-voiced narrator over side-by-side photos, "please note that César Chávez (right) fought for migrant workers' rights in California and has no connection to Venezuela. Hugo Chávez (left) was our former president who died in 2013. Nicolás Maduro (center) is our current president. None of them controls America's lettuce supply."

In the upscale Caracas neighborhood of Altamira, renowned Venezuelan chef Carmen Fernandez was hosting an emergency meeting of the country's top culinary experts.

"Trump specifically mentioned arepas as 'unfair foreign competition to American pancakes' and accused us of 'corn-based breakfast imperialism,'" she explained to the assembled chefs and food producers.

"But arepas aren't even remotely similar to pancakes!" protested a baker famous for his traditional Venezuelan breads.

"And the corn for our arepas comes from American imports!" added another chef.

In a perplexed State Department, an official was attempting to explain to Trump the multiple layers of confusion in his Venezuelan tariff policy.

"Sir, César Chávez was an American civil rights activist who organized farm workers in the United States. He passed away in 1993 and never had any connection to Venezuela."

Trump's eyes narrowed suspiciously. "So you're telling me there are THREE Chavezes now? Hugo, César, and Nicholas? Very sneaky. Probably all related. A Chavez dynasty controlling all the lettuce and grapes. Bad hombres, all of them."

As evening fell across Caracas, at a small family-owned arepa restaurant, seventy-year-old Guadalupe Rincón was explaining the situation to her grandchildren as she patted corn dough into perfect circles.

"When I was a girl," she said, skillfully flipping an arepa on the griddle, "we worried about military coups and political revolutions. Now we worry about an American president who thinks our arepas are secretly pancakes sent to destroy capitalism."

Her teenage grandson looked up from his phone. "Abuela, Trump just tweeted that he wants to build a wall around the United States to keep Venezuelan avocados out."

"But our avocados don't even—" She stopped mid-sentence and shook her head, a wry smile forming on her weathered face. "Muchacho, in Venezuela, we have a saying: 'La vida es una arepa – puedes llorar por lo que falta, o disfrutar lo que tienes.'"

"Life is like an arepa – you can cry over what's missing, or enjoy what you have," her grandson translated.

"Exactly," she said, sliding a perfectly golden arepa onto his plate. "And what we have is delicious, with or without Trump's approval."

As President Maduro addressed the nation that evening, he stood before a gigantic triptych of himself, Hugo Chávez, and César Chávez with large red X's between them.

"Citizens of Venezuela! The United States has once again attacked our sovereignty, this time with tariffs based on a confusion worthy of a bad telenovela. For clarity: I am Nicolás Maduro, your president. I am not Hugo Chávez. I am not César Chávez. And none of us is plotting an agricultural invasion of America."

Chapter 18
The Great TikTok Tariff Crisis

When the White House announced a 40% "Digital Culture Tariff" on TikTok, most Americans over 40 responded with confusion, vague concerns about China, and the lingering suspicion that TikTok was either a breath mint or something their grandchildren did in bedrooms with doors suspiciously locked.

For Generation Z, however, the news triggered an apocalypse that made climate change look like a minor inconvenience.

"This is literally the end of civilization," declared 19-year-old influencer Madison "MaddieSlayz" Thompson to her 3.7 million followers while performing a perfectly choreographed dance that somehow conveyed existential despair through hip movements. "Trump doesn't understand that TikTok isn't just an app—it's, like, our entire economic system?"

Indeed, what Senate committees dismissively called "kids making silly dances" had evolved into a shadow economy where teenagers earned more posting fifteen-second videos than their parents made in careers requiring advanced degrees and soul-crushing commutes.

The tariff—calculated by combining TikTok's daily active users, the average number of hashtags per post, and Trump's personal irritation at not understanding the platform—would supposedly be paid by the Chinese parent company. In reality, TikTok announced it would reduce creator payments by exactly 40%, sending influencer mansions across Los Angeles into unprecedented panic.

"I just bought a Lamborghini based on my projected earnings from the 'Devious Lick' dance trend," lamented 17-year-old Trevor "TrevDripz" Williams in a tearful video that somehow still incorporated perfect lighting and three product placements. "Now I'll have to return it and get, like, a regular luxury car like some kind of millennial."

White House Press Secretary Karoline Leavitt attempted to explain the tariff's purpose to a room full of journalists who still primarily consumed news through actual reading.

"TikTok represents unfair competition to American attention spans," she announced. "The President believes American social media companies should have priority access to our citizens' rapidly diminishing capacity for focus."

When a 23-year-old reporter from BuzzFeed asked how a tariff on a free app would work, Leavitt suggested she "Google it."

The most effective resistance came from an unexpected alliance: grandparents and their Gen Z grandchildren. Across America, teens taught their grandparents to post anti-tariff content, resulting in a viral tsunami of confused elderly people inadvertently creating perfect comedic timing through technological incompetence.

"MY GRANDSON SAYS TICTACS WILL COST MORE," wrote 87-year-old Edith Pemberton in a text overlay while pointing confusedly above her head where no text actually appeared. "THIS IS AN OUTRAGE I NEED THEM FOR MY DIGESTION." The video received 14 million views and sparked the trend #GrandparentsAgainstTariffs.

Tech executives, seeing opportunity in chaos, rushed to create domestic alternatives. Mark Zuckerberg announced "American Dance Party," an identical clone of TikTok that came pre-installed with patriotic filters and what he called "constitutionally protected data harvesting."

Trump himself attempted to join the conversation, posting a video that consisted entirely of him pointing at the camera for 60 uncomfortable seconds while "God Bless the USA" played at distorted volume levels. The clip was immediately remixed into the "Authoritarian Shuffle" dance craze that swept middle schools nationwide.

In a final twist, the Treasury Department discovered it had no actual mechanism to collect the tariff since TikTok was a free service. Their solution—requiring users to Venmo the government 40% of any earnings—was abandoned after realizing it would require hiring 500,000 new IRS agents specifically to track dance-based income.

The tariff was ultimately rescinded after National Security officials discovered that three of their most valuable intelligence sources on Chinese activities were actually just teenagers in New Jersey doing impersonations while reviewing bubble tea flavors.

As 16-year-old influencer Zoe "ZoZo" Zhang put it in a video that somehow explained complex international trade policy while applying perfect winged eyeliner: "Imagine thinking you can put a tariff on culture. That's so 2019. Literally no one taxes vibes."

Chapter 19

Brazil: Samba Economics

President Luiz Inácio Lula da Silva was enjoying his morning cafezinho on the Palácio da Alvorada terrace when his trade minister burst in, clutching his phone with the panic of a man who had just seen Cristo Redentor do the samba.

"Presidente! Trump has imposed a 43% tariff on all Brazilian exports!"

Lula took an unhurried sip of his intensely dark coffee. After survivng prison, cancer, and eight presidential elections, news of American tariffs barely registered on his crisis meter.

"Quanto?" he asked calmly. "Forty-three percent? Not even a round number? Typical American inefficiency."

The trade minister thrust his phone forward, displaying the official White House announcement. "According to our economists, Trump appears to have calculated our tariff rate by combining the number of Brazilian goals in the 1970 World Cup, the average annual rainfall in the Amazon in inches, and the total number of feathers on a standard Carnival headdress, divided by the temperature of the average caipirinha."

Lula chuckled, setting down his tiny coffee cup. "And they say our approach to mathematics is creative. Tell me, what reason has he given for this... economic poetry?"

"He claims Brazil has an 'unfair climate advantage' that makes our crops grow faster, 'excessive soccer skills' that create unfair competition for American athletes, and 'too many beautiful people' which constitutes a 'major distraction to American productivity.'"

In the bustling finance ministry in Brasília, where ceiling fans turned lazily despite the building's supposedly modern air conditioning, Minister Fernando Haddad was addressing a crisis meeting that somehow resembled a neighborhood barbecue more than a government summit.

"The Americans have finally lost their minds completely," he announced to his team, who were simultaneously typing on laptops, arguing passionately, and passing around a plate of pão de queijo. "Trump believes our coffee has an 'unfair caffeine advantage' over American coffee because—and this is a direct quote—'Brazilian beans get more sunlight which makes them more caffeinated.'"

"But that's not how caffeine works," protested a junior economist.

"Explaining science to Trump is like teaching a capybara to play chess," replied Haddad. "Theoretically possible, but why waste everyone's time?"

In Rio de Janeiro, the tariff news was received with Brazil's trademark blend of fatalism and irreverence. At Copacabana Beach, surf instructor Paulo Coelho (no relation to the author) philosophized to his students as they watched waves crash against the shore.

"Americans think they can control everything with rules and taxes," he mused, expertly balancing on one foot while applying sunscreen to his impossibly perfect abs. "But Brazil has survived dictators, hyperinflation, and seven consecutive World Cup disappointments. We have a saying here: 'Deus é brasileiro'—God is Brazilian. He'll think of something."

In the Amazon, where illegal loggers momentarily paused their chainsaws upon hearing the tariff news, indigenous leader Raoni Metuktire offered perhaps the most insightful analysis.

"The white man in America taxes our açaí berries because they are too healthy, our coffee because it is too good, and our wood because our trees are too tall," he observed to a visiting anthropologist. "Perhaps if they spent less time counting money and more time planting trees, they wouldn't need to punish others for having forests."

Meanwhile, in the industrial hub of São Paulo, business leaders gathered at the Federation of Industries to formulate a response. Unlike their European counterparts, who would have prepared detailed PowerPoints and economic projections, the Brazilian industrialists approached the crisis with the same improvisational flair they applied to everything from business deals to traffic laws.

"We'll just relabel everything as 'Made in Paraguay' and ship it through Uruguay," suggested one manufacturing magnate, to general approval.

"Or we could declare all our exports 'Carnival supplies' – Americans never tax anything related to parties," offered another.

The head of Brazil's massive meatpacking industry had an even more direct solution: "We simply invite Trump to Brazil. Three days of beaches, barbecue, and beautiful people, and he'll forget all about tariffs."

In Washington, Trump was explaining his Brazilian tariff decision to befuddled economists.

"Brazil has been very, very unfair to us on climate," Trump declared, gesturing to a map where the entire Amazon rainforest had been circled in red marker. "They have all these trees making oxygen, the best oxygen, and they're not sharing the profits with America. Plus, their beaches make our beaches look terrible. Very unfair beach advantage."

When a University of Chicago economist attempted to explain that oxygen doesn't generate profit and beach quality isn't a trade issue, Trump waved dismissively.

"Brazil grows all these things—coffee, sugarcane, soybeans—much faster than we do because they have this special soil. Very suspicious soil. They should share this soil technology with American farmers."

Back in Brazil, President Lula had assembled his response team, which—in typical Brazilian fashion—included economists, diplomats, a soccer legend, a Carnival dancer, and his personal barbecue chef.

"The Americans expect us to panic," Lula explained, as his team arrayed themselves around a table laden with tropical fruits, grilled meats, and economic briefing documents. "They forget we invented the concept of 'jeitinho brasileiro'—finding the creative way around every problem."

"We'll respond to these tariffs the Brazilian way," he continued with a smile. "We'll complain loudly, ignore them creatively, adapt immediately, and invite everyone to a party where we'll solve everything over caipirinhas."

As his cabinet nodded in agreement, Lula raised his coffee cup in a toast: "Besides, Trump clearly doesn't understand one fundamental truth about Brazil: We already tax ourselves at rates that make his tariffs look like a tip at a cheap restaurant. After surviving our own bureaucracy, American tariffs are just samba music to our ears."

Chapter 20
Israel: The Chosen Tariff

Prime Minister Benjamin Netanyahu was in the middle of his third coalition crisis that week when his security briefing was interrupted with news that Trump had imposed a 27% tariff on all Israeli exports.

"Nu? That's it?" Netanyahu shrugged with characteristic Israeli dismissal of what others might consider a catastrophe. "From the way you rushed in, I thought Hamas had taken over the Knesset cafeteria."

His economic advisor, a former Mossad agent who'd once neutralized an Iranian nuclear scientist using only a PowerPoint presentation, pushed forward a tablet displaying the official White House tariff announcement.

"It's not the percentage that concerns me, sir," the advisor explained. "It's Trump's justification. He's claiming Israeli tech companies have an 'unfair intelligence advantage' because, and I quote directly, 'their programmers all did spy stuff in the army.'"

Netanyahu adjusted his tie, a gesture he'd perfected through decades of explaining to Americans why their suggestions about Middle East peace were completely detached from reality.

"Trump thinks our military service gives us an unfair advantage?" The Prime Minister permitted himself a small smile. "Wait until he discovers our mothers. Now *that's* an advantage no tariff can neutralize."

Within hours, Israel's response machine was operating with the efficiency that comes from existential threats being a Tuesday. In the Defense Ministry, where every office featured at least three exit strategies and a weapon hidden in a desk drawer, military officials were already analyzing the tariff as if it were an incoming missile.

"The Americans have clearly lost their minds," declared Defense Minister Yoav Gallant, studying the tariff documentation while simultaneously approving a drone strike and texting his wife about dinner plans. "But this is hardly the first time. Remember when they suggested we just 'talk it out' with Hezbollah?"

In the gleaming high-rises of Tel Aviv's tech district, Israel's startup community was having a markedly different reaction. At the headquarters of CyberChutzpah, a cybersecurity firm whose main office featured beanbag chairs, emotional support dogs, and enough hidden surveillance equipment to monitor a small nation, CEO Sarah Goldstein addressed her team.

"Trump thinks our military experience gives us an unfair advantage in tech?" she asked, standing in front of a wall of monitors. "He's not wrong. But he's forgetting something crucial—Israelis invented the concept of the workaround."

Her team, an eclectic mix of secular Jews in startup t-shirts, a few Arabs who'd graduated from the Technion, and one ultra-Orthodox programmer who'd convinced his rabbi that writing code was essentially the same as studying Talmud, nodded in agreement.

"We'll just rename the company, run everything through a subsidiary in Liechtenstein, and add American flag emojis to all our emails," suggested the head of marketing, who'd once convinced the Egyptian border patrol that his drone was actually a uniquely shaped selfie stick.

Meanwhile, in Jerusalem's ultra-Orthodox neighborhood of Mea Shearim, a different sort of emergency meeting was taking place. In a study hall where internet-connected devices were theoretically forbidden (though everyone mysteriously received the news within minutes), black-hatted men debated the tariffs with the same intensity normally reserved for Talmudic discussions.

"It's clearly stated in Bava Metzia 44a that artificial price controls disrupt God's divine market," argued one rabbi, swaying slightly as he spoke. "Trump's tariffs contradict the teachings of Maimonides on fair commerce!"

"But what about our diamond exports?" countered another, stroking his beard with concern. "The Americans buy most of our gemstones!"

A younger Hasidic man looked up from a suspiciously smartphone-shaped volume of religious texts. "Perhaps we could declare the diamonds religious artifacts? Americans never question anything labeled 'religious freedom.'"

Across town in the colorful Mahane Yehuda market, everyday Israelis responded with their characteristic blend of fatalism, improvisation, and aggressive negotiation tactics.

"Twenty-seven percent tariff? That's nothing!" shouted Abu Sameer, a fruit vendor whose family had been selling pomegranates in the same spot since the Ottoman Empire. "I'll give you thirty percent off these grapes, forty percent off the dates, and throw in some free hummus if you buy now! But only for you, because you have a nice face."

When informed the tariff was something America was charging Israel, not a discount, Abu Sameer shrugged. "So they learned to negotiate like Israelis. About time!"

At a nearby café, where three separate customers were visibly carrying assault rifles while casually eating shakshuka, a heated debate had broken out about the most efficient way to deal with Trump.

"We should send in the Mossad," suggested a former paratrooper, now a philosophy student, gesturing emphatically with a fork. "One good operation, he drops the tariffs, no one knows what happened."

"Too messy," countered his companion, a tech worker who'd completed her military service in an intelligence unit so secret even she wasn't sure what it did. "We should just hack his Twitter and make him announce that Israel is exempt because we're 'tremendously good allies, the best allies.'"

An elderly man at the next table lowered his newspaper. "You're all thinking too hard. Just send his son-in-law Kushner some WhatsApp messages. Isn't he Jewish? Problem solved."

In Washington, Trump was explaining his Israeli tariff decision to bewildered reporters.

"Israel has been very unfair to us on technology," Trump declared, gesturing to a chart showing Israeli innovation statistics.

"They have all these startups, tremendous startups, but they don't make things you can touch. It's all 'cyber' this and 'algorithm' that. I like stuff you can hold. Big, beautiful physical things."

When a reporter pointed out that many American tech companies also focus on software rather than physical products, Trump waved dismissively.

"Different situation. Completely different. Israel has this unfair advantage because every kid goes into the army and learns computer tricks. Very unfair to American kids who spend those years on Instagram."

Back in Jerusalem, Netanyahu was on a secure line with Trump, employing Israel's time-tested diplomatic strategy: agree enthusiastically, then do exactly what you were going to do anyway.

"Donald, my friend, you're absolutely right about everything," Netanyahu cooed, while simultaneously signing orders to circumvent the tariffs through a byzantine network of shell companies. "The strongest relationship in history, Israel and America. You know, we're naming a settlement after you right now. Trump Heights. Very luxurious settlement. The best."

As Netanyahu continued sweet-talking the American president, his economic team was already executing a multi-pronged response:

1. Israeli tech companies would officially rename their products to include "AMERICAN PARTNERSHIP" in the title

2. Military intelligence would compile a dossier on every U.S. customs official responsible for tariff enforcement

3. A new Mossad unit would focus exclusively on hunting down Nazi gold to offset tariff losses

Within three days, Israel had completely reorganized its export strategy, found seventeen legal loopholes in the tariff legislation, and somehow managed to increase its exports to America by 12%.

"This is hardly our biggest problem," Netanyahu told his cabinet as they finalized the response. "I've got three coalition partners threatening to quit over whether the Knesset cafeteria should serve milk and meat on the same day, Iran is enriching uranium, and my trial resumes on Tuesday. A little tariff? This is what we call in Hebrew a 'Tuesday morning warm-up exercise.'"

As night fell over Jerusalem, the eternal city that had survived empires, crusades, and countless foreign policies, life continued largely unchanged. In a typical Israeli response to crisis, people argued passionately about the tariffs, offered seventeen different solutions (all presented as the only possible option), and then went about their business with the calm of a people who measure existential threats on a relative scale.

As one Tel Aviv bartender put it to an American tourist who asked about the tariffs: "Trump thinks he can pressure Israel with economics? Cute. Call me when he surrounds us with tanks. Actually, don't bother—we've handled that before too."

Chapter 21
Saudi Arabia: The Royal Tariff

Crown Prince Mohammed bin Salman was enjoying a quiet morning in his 600-room palace, scrolling through the latest $500 billion city designs on his gold-plated iPad, when his finance minister approached with the sort of hesitation typically reserved for announcing that one had accidentally misplaced the Kaaba.

"Your Royal Highness," the minister began, bowing deeply, "I regret to inform you that American President Trump has imposed a 26% tariff on all Saudi exports."

The Crown Prince, known to the world as MBS, didn't immediately look up from his iPad, where he was considering whether the artificial moon for his new desert megacity should be merely enormous or truly excessive.

"Twenty-six percent?" he finally replied, his tone more curious than concerned. "On oil?"

"Yes, Your Highness. On oil, petrochemicals, and..." the minister checked his notes, "...dates."

At this, MBS set down his tablet. A tariff on oil was one thing, but dates? That was personal.

"What explanation has Trump given for this... imposition?" MBS asked, the last word carrying the quiet menace of someone who hadn't heard the word "no" since his third birthday.

The finance minister swallowed hard. "According to the White House statement, Saudi Arabia has an 'unfair sandy advantage' and 'too much oil for one country.' Trump also mentioned that our buildings are 'suspiciously shiny.'"

MBS stood, adjusting his pristine white thobe with the precision of a man who employed sixteen people just to manage his wardrobe. "Call an emergency meeting of the Royal Council. And inform the Sovereign Wealth Fund managers. I wish to purchase... something American."

Within hours, the Saudi Royal Council had assembled in a conference room featuring more gold than Fort Knox and a chandelier that had its own dedicated cleaning staff. Unlike democratic nations where economic crises prompted heated debate, the Saudi response was characterized by absolute deference to MBS, occasionally interrupted by someone suggesting even more extreme displays of wealth.

"The American tariffs are clearly based on jealousy," declared the Minister of Economy, careful to make his observation sound like agreement with whatever MBS might have been thinking. "They wish their desert had oil instead of just... desert."

"Perhaps we should remind Trump who purchases his condominiums?" suggested the Foreign Minister delicately.

MBS silenced the room with a raised eyebrow, an expression he had practiced for hours in front of titanium mirrors imported from Switzerland.

"Gentlemen, Trump has clearly forgotten whom he is dealing with. We are Saudi Arabia. We do not negotiate with tariffs. We buy our way around them."

He turned to his chief economic advisor. "What is the projected annual impact of this tariff?"

"Approximately $7 billion, Your Highness."

MBS nodded thoughtfully. "And what is our daily oil revenue?"

"Approximately $1 billion, Your Highness."

"So this tariff will cost us... one week of oil revenue?" MBS clarified, the concept of financial constraint as foreign to him as public transportation.

"Essentially, yes."

MBS smiled. "Then we shall barely notice it. However, it is the principle that concerns me. Americans cannot simply tax the Kingdom. Prepare three responses."

The council waited expectantly.

"First, inform our sovereign wealth fund to identify an American company that Trump particularly likes, and buy it. Something visible and unnecessary."

"Twitter, Your Highness?" suggested the investment minister.

"Been done. Something more... Trump. Perhaps a golf equipment manufacturer? Or a company that makes those little American flags for suits?"

"Second," MBS continued, "accelerate construction of The Line."

The Line was Saudi Arabia's most ambitious project yet—a 170-kilometer mirrored city in the desert with no roads, cars, or emissions, designed to house nine million people in what architects quietly referred to as "possibly the most expensive hallway in human history."

"When complete, we will offer Trump a golden apartment in The Line, where he can admire his reflection infinitely in both directions. This will distract him from tariffs."

The council nodded appreciatively at this sophisticated psychological warfare.

"And third," MBS concluded, "inform Trump that we are considering yuan-based oil trades with China."

This last directive sent a shiver through the room. Playing the China card was the Saudi equivalent of flipping the chess board.

Meanwhile, in NEOM, the futuristic region being constructed along the Red Sea coast, Saudi planners were already adapting their designs to incorporate tariff-response elements. The project director, Prince Khalid bin Salman, addressed his team of international architects and engineers via holographic conference call from his yacht anchored off the Maldives.

"Gentlemen, we must adjust our flying car infrastructure to account for American tariffs," the Prince announced to his bewildered team. "If America wishes to tax our oil, we shall simply build a city that requires none."

An American architect tentatively raised his hand. "Your Highness, NEOM was already designed to be zero-carbon. That was the entire concept."

The Prince waved dismissively. "Yes, but now we must make it anti-tariff as well. Add more mirrors. Trump likes mirrors. And perhaps a Trump Tower, but taller, shinier, and with more gold. This will confuse him."

Across the Kingdom, Saudi citizens responded to news of the tariffs with the characteristic blend of pride and pragmatism that came from being subjects in one of the world's wealthiest absolute monarchies.

At a luxury café in Riyadh, where the coffee was infused with saffron and actual gold flakes, businessman Faisal al-Saud (no relation to the royal family, though he did nothing to discourage the assumption) discussed the tariffs with colleagues.

"Trump thinks he can pressure us with economics?" Faisal laughed. "The Kingdom bought $7 billion in superyachts just last year. For weekend use."

His companion, recently returned from studying at Harvard, nodded thoughtfully. "It's not about the money. It's about the respect. The Americans forget that we can simply... turn off the tap."

In Washington, Trump was explaining his Saudi tariff strategy with his usual diplomatic finesse.

"Saudi Arabia has been very unfair to us on sand," Trump declared, pointing to a chart comparing American and Saudi sand reserves. "They have the best sand, tremendous sand. Our sand is garbage sand, mostly in New Jersey. Very sad."

When a Wall Street Journal reporter pointed out that sand wasn't a major Saudi export to America, Trump waved dismissively.

"It's not about the sand, it's about the principle. They have too much oil, which is under the sand. Very suspicious arrangement. Nobody needs that much oil except America."

Back in Riyadh, MBS received word that Trump was unmoved by initial Saudi responses. The Crown Prince smiled the serene smile of someone whose personal net worth exceeded the GDP of 75% of the world's nations.

"If Trump wants to play games with tariffs, we shall show him how we play in the Kingdom," he announced to his advisors. "Prepare the royal aircraft. Load it with our finest dates, three Lamborghinis, and one of the smaller Picassos. We shall pay Trump a royal visit."

When an advisor delicately asked what message this would send, MBS's smile broadened.

"In America, power is measured in tweets and tariffs. In Saudi Arabia, power is measured in how casually one can give away Lamborghinis. We shall speak to Trump in the only language that transcends all cultures: excessive displays of wealth."

As the 747 was being loaded with luxury cars and priceless art, MBS added a final instruction: "And prepare a solid gold model of The Line. If Trump wishes to tax our exports, we shall simply build a new world and invite him to visit. For a reasonable fee, of course. Say, 26%?"

Chapter 22

The Final Slot

Making Grand Fenwick Great Again

The atmosphere in the White House Situation Room was tense as President Trump's economic advisors, cabinet members, and assorted staffers huddled around the massive "GLOBAL TARIFF MASTER CHART" that now covered an entire wall. After weeks of imposing tariffs on every identifiable nation, territory, and semi-autonomous region on Earth, they had reached a critical juncture.

"Mr. President," announced Treasury Secretary Scott Bessent, pointing to a single empty slot at the bottom of the chart, "we have room for exactly one more country on the tariff schedule."

Trump, who had been doodling tariff percentages on his notepad, perked up immediately. "Fantastic! Let's make it a good one. The best one. Who haven't we tariffed yet?"

Commerce Secretary Howard Lutnick consulted his tablet. "Actually, sir, we've covered all 195 recognized sovereign states, plus 72 dependent territories, 5 disputed territories, 4 uninhabited Antarctic islands, and Puerto Rico, which is technically part of the United States."

"What about that little country shaped like a boot?" Trump asked.

"Italy, sir. Already hit with 18%."

"The one with all the chocolate and cuckoo clocks?"

"Switzerland. 19.5%."

Trump frowned, tapping his pen against the table. "There must be something we missed. A sneaky little country hiding somewhere. Maybe one of those places with a funny name nobody can pronounce."

Vice President JD Vance cleared his throat. "What about the Duchy of Grand Fenwick, sir?"

The room fell silent. White House Chief of Staff Susie Wiles shot Vance a warning look, but it was too late.

"Grand Fenwick!" Trump's eyes lit up. "I knew we were forgetting one! Where is that again? Sounds European. Very sneaky, very European."

Secretary of State Marco Rubio looked confused. "Sir, I don't believe there is a country called—"

"Of course there is!" Trump interrupted. "Duchy of Grand Fenwick. They make wine or watches or something. Probably both. Taking advantage of us for years. Nobody talks about it. Sad!"

The assembled advisors exchanged nervous glances. National Security Advisor Mike Waltz leaned over to whisper to Rubio, "Should someone tell him Grand Fenwick doesn't exist? It's from that old Peter Sellers movie."

Rubio shook his head slightly. "Last guy who corrected his geography was fired via Twitter while in the bathroom."

Trump was now enthusiastically circling the empty slot on the tariff chart. "Grand Fenwick gets the final spot! What should we charge them? I'm thinking 40%. They sound fancy with that 'Duchy' business. Very elitist. Probably looking down on us."

Economic advisor Kevin Hassett tentatively raised a hand. "Mr. President, I'm not certain we can impose tariffs on Grand Fenwick because—"

"Because they're too small?" Trump cut in. "Size doesn't matter. We tariffed Liechtenstein, right? Tiny place. Barely visible on a map. But they still pay!"

"No, sir," Hassett continued carefully, "it's because Grand Fenwick is a fictional country from a 1955 novel and 1959 film called 'The Mouse That Roared.' It doesn't actually exist."

Trump stared at Hassett for a long, uncomfortable moment before breaking into laughter. "Good one, Kevin! Next you'll tell me Finland isn't real either!" He turned to Vance. "JD knows about Grand Fenwick. Right, JD?"

Put on the spot, Vance nodded solemnly. "Indeed, Mr. President. The Duchy of Grand Fenwick is... a very real place that has been taking advantage of our trade policies for decades."

"Exactly!" Trump slammed his hand on the table. "They've been flying under the radar. Very sneaky. But no country escapes our tariffs. Not even sneaky Grand Fenwick!"

An aide passed Trump a note. He read it, frowning. "It says here Grand Fenwick's main export is... pinot noir wine? And they have a standing army of 20 longbow archers?" He looked up, puzzled. "Is that right?"

"Absolutely correct, sir," Vance confirmed with a straight face. "They're known for their medieval military traditions and exceptional wine production."

Trump nodded, satisfied. "Wine tariffs it is! 40% on Grand Fenwick wine!"

As the meeting proceeded, staffers were dispatched to create an official-looking profile of the Duchy of Grand Fenwick, complete with fabricated trade statistics, a hastily photoshopped flag (Switzerland's with clip art of a mouse added), and population figures described as "probably small, but very devious."

By evening, Fox News was running a special segment titled "Grand Fenwick: The Tiny European Nation Undermining American Wine," featuring interviews with "experts" who were actually White House interns speaking in fake accents.

At the Treasury Department, panicked officials tried to create customs codes for "Grand Fenwickian imports" while a team at the State Department debated whether they needed to establish a diplomatic outreach to a fictional nation.

Three days later, Trump hosted a special signing ceremony for the "Grand Fenwick Fair Trade Executive Order," which included a 40% tariff on "all goods and services originating from or passing through the Duchy of Grand Fenwick."

As cameras flashed, a reporter from the Washington Post hesitantly raised her hand. "Mr. President, Grand Fenwick is a fictional country from a comedy film. It doesn't actually exist."

Trump's smile vanished. "Fake news! Just because you've never heard of Grand Fenwick doesn't mean it's not real. They're small but very real. I have an excellent relationship with their leader... Duke Ferdinand or whatever."

"But sir, it's literally from a movie starring Peter Sellers. It was created by a novelist."

Trump turned to Secretary of Defense Pete Hegseth. "Pete, show her the Grand Fenwick file."

Hegseth reluctantly handed over a folder containing what appeared to be official intelligence on Grand Fenwick, including maps that were clearly screenshots from the movie with Microsoft Paint additions.

"As you can see," Trump continued smugly, "very real place. Great people. Making great wines. But unfair to America. Now they'll pay their fair share."

That evening, White House staffers added the final touches to the Global Tariff Master Chart: "Duchy of Grand Fenwick - 40%" written in gold Sharpie at the bottom.

As news of the Grand Fenwick tariff spread, a strange thing happened. Wines began appearing in liquor stores around the country labeled as "Genuine Duchy of Grand Fenwick Reserve"—actually cheap California wines with fancy new labels. Hipster bars in Brooklyn started serving "Grand Fenwickian cocktails." Someone even opened a "Grand Fenwick Trade Commission" office in Washington D.C., which was actually just a postal box that collected "tariff payments" from people who thought it would be funny to mail in monopoly money.

When informed that people were paying fake tariffs on products from a fake country, Trump declared it "the most successful tariff in American history" and ordered a commemorative coin to be minted featuring his face on one side and the made-up Grand Fenwickian coat of arms on the other.

Six months later, the Treasury Department quietly admitted that the Grand Fenwick tariff had somehow generated $2.3 million in revenue, proving once and for all that in Trump's America, even imaginary countries could be bullied into paying their fair share.

Chapter 23
Madagascar: The Vanilla Wars

"VANILLA IS THE NEW NUCLEAR," declared the bright red chyron scrolling across Fox News as a stern-faced Tucker Carlson 2.0—an AI hologram that replaced the original after his mysterious disappearance to Russia—stared intensely into the camera. "Is your ice cream funding TERRORISM? President Trump thinks SO."

President Andry Rajoelina of Madagascar was enjoying his morning breakfast of vanilla-infused coffee when his phone exploded. Not literally, though that would have been less shocking than the notification banner: "BREAKING: U.S. DECLARES VANILLA A CONTROLLED SUBSTANCE, IMPOSES 47% TARIFF ON MADAGASCAR."

"Forty-seven percent?" he sputtered, spraying coffee across his economic minister's pristine white shirt. "Why not just make it 50%? Or 100%? Or a billion percent? Has Trump ever actually looked at Madagascar on a map?"

The economic minister dabbed at his ruined shirt. "Sir, according to our intelligence, Trump believes Madagascar is the animated film. Yesterday he tweeted that our 'talking lions and dancing hippos' represent unfair competition to American zoo animals."

Meanwhile, in the Oval Office, Trump was holding court with his new cabinet of economic advisors, all of whom suspiciously resembled his former caddies.

"Madagascar," Trump announced, jabbing his finger at a map that was actually a Denny's placemat featuring cartoon animals from around the world, "is absolutely KILLING us on vanilla. KILLING US DEAD. They're using unfair tactics like... like... whatdayacallit?"

"Tropical weather, sir?" offered Commerce Secretary Howard Lutnick.

"EXACTLY! Totally unfair. We can't grow vanilla in Nebraska because they've hoarded all the good weather. It's weather manipulation. Probably Chinese technology involved."

Back in Madagascar, in the tiny village of Ambohimiarina, vanilla farmer Haja Rasoanaivo stared at her phone in disbelief as her American buyer canceled $30,000 worth of orders. Around her stretched acres of meticulously tended vanilla vines, each flower hand-pollinated in a process so delicate it made brain surgery look like sledgehammer practice.

"Yesterday I was just a farmer," she told her assembled family. "Today I am apparently an economic supervillain."

Her eldest son looked up from his economics textbook. "But mother, Madagascar's entire GDP is less than what America spends on pet costumes each year."

"Clearly our vanilla is more powerful than we realized," she replied dryly. "Perhaps we should start charging warfare prices."

In Washington, the Treasury Department unveiled its new "Vanilla Security Threat Level Indicator"—a giant ice cream cone on the White House lawn that changed colors based on perceived vanilla-related threats. It was currently set to "Fudge Ripple Red."

Secretary of Defense Pete Hegseth announced a new military branch: the "Vanilla Special Operations Command," tasked with intercepting suspicious orchid shipments. Their logo featured an eagle clutching a vanilla bean while screaming patriotically.

The administration released a 700-page report titled "The Vanilla Menace: Madagascar's Flavor Hegemony and the Threat to American Desserts," which primarily consisted of ice cream recipes interspersed with random ALL-CAPS warnings about "FOREIGN FLAVOR INTERFERENCE."

President Trump, addressing reporters while eating from a gallon tub of artificially flavored "PATRIOT VANILLA" ice cream, explained his economic philosophy: "Look, we're losing to Madagascar bigly. Their vanilla farmers—some of them, I assume, are good people—but they're laughing at us. Just yesterday, a very strong, very tough vanilla farmer—big guy, tears in his eyes—said 'Sir, thank you for finally standing up to BIG VANILLA.'"

Vice President JD Vance solemnly nodded beside him, holding a vanilla milkshake with a tiny American flag stuck in it. "What people don't understand is that vanilla is about American values. Every time you lick foreign vanilla ice cream, you're basically burning the Constitution."

In Madagascar's capital, creative resistance was already forming. The Minister of Agriculture unveiled "Freedom Vanilla"—identical to regular vanilla but shipped in patriotic red, white, and blue packaging featuring bald eagles. "Now with 47% more American spirit!" the label promised.

Enterprising farmers began classifying their vanilla as "Tactical Flavor Enhancement Modules" to bypass tariff regulations.

The Madagascar Vanilla Cooperative published a full-page ad in the New York Times, featuring a photo of a tiny 12-year-old girl carefully pollinating a vanilla orchid. The headline read: "BEHOLD THE FACE OF AMERICA'S GREATEST ECONOMIC RIVAL. TREMBLE BEFORE HER TINY POLLINATION STICK."

As global ice cream prices tripled overnight, causing riots outside Ben & Jerry's locations worldwide, Madagascar's president finally issued an official response. It was simply a photo of a vanilla flower with the caption: "This declaration of economic war has left us utterly flabbergasted. We would invite President Trump to visit Madagascar, but we fear he might try to arrest our lemurs for espionage."

The White House immediately classified lemurs as "furry economic combatants" and banned all Madagascar-related content on Netflix. The animated film "Madagascar" was digitally altered to replace all animal characters with paintings of Trump crossing the Delaware.

In a final insult, the tariff's implementation date - April 9th - happened to coincide with Madagascar's National Vanilla Day, a holiday that didn't actually exist until Malagasy officials created it specifically to spite Trump.

Chapter 24
Nigeria: URGENT BUSINESS PROPOSAL

FROM: His Royal Highness Prince Adebayo Adeyemi Afolayan
**MINISTRY OF TARIFF AFFAIRS & EXPORT
ROYALTIES Federal Republic of Nigeria**

STRICTLY CONFIDENTIAL / URGENT BUSINESS
PROPOSAL

Dear Respected American Sir/Madam,

Permit me to introduce myself. I am HRH PRINCE ADE-
BAYO ADEYEMI AFOLAYAN, the eldest son of the late KING
ADEYEMI IV of the OYO KINGDOM and CHAIRMAN of
the NIGERIAN TARIFF CIRCUMVENTION COMMIT-
TEE. I write to you with tears in my eyes regarding the recent imposition of UNFAIR 44% TARIFFS upon my kingdom's exports
by YOUR PRESIDENT DONALD TRUMP.

I came upon your email address through divine guidance and
the UNITED STATES CUSTOMS & BORDER PROTEC-
TION DIRECTORY. I have been searching for a trustwor-
thy American ally to assist in a MUTUALLY BENEFICIAL
TRANSACTION of most urgent and confidential nature.

As you may be aware, President Trump has imposed PUNI-
TIVE TARIFFS on Nigerian exports including OIL, COCOA,
and ROYAL CEREMONIAL LEOPARD SKINS. He claims
Nigeria has "UNFAIR ADVANTAGE in natural resources" and
"SUSPICIOUS number of princes." These tariffs have frozen
$45,600,000.00 (FORTY-FIVE MILLION SIX HUNDRED
THOUSAND US DOLLARS) of my family's export revenue in
AMERICAN CUSTOMS ESCROW ACCOUNTS.

My intelligence sources have confirmed that Trump calculated
our tariff percentage by combining:

1. The number of emails sent by Nigerian princes in 2023

2. The average temperature of Lagos in Fahrenheit

3. The total weight in pounds of ceremonial gold in the royal
   palace

4. Minus the number of Nigerian NBA players

Our royal mathematicians have verified this is COMPLETELY NONSENSICAL.

Due to unfortunate diplomatic circumstances and the ALLEGED involvement of my half-brother in a TOTALLY FABRICATED scheme involving iTunes gift cards, we cannot access these funds directly. This is where YOU, as an AMERICAN CITIZEN OF GOOD STANDING, enter the picture.

MY PROPOSITION: With your assistance as a TARIFF EXEMPTION CONSULTANT, we can reclassify our exports as "EDUCATIONAL MATERIALS" and "RELIGIOUS ARTIFACTS" which are exempt from President Trump's tariff schedule according to provision 419.B of the INTERNATIONAL TRADE ACT.

For your cooperation and bank account details, I am prepared to offer you 30% of the recovered funds, totaling $13,680,000.00 (THIRTEEN MILLION SIX HUNDRED EIGHTY THOUSAND US DOLLARS). I have also secured permission from the ANCESTRAL COUNCIL to include a BONUS GIFT of THREE (3) CEREMONIAL LEOPARD CUBS and ONE (1) GOVERNMENT MINISTRY POSITION (your choice of ministry).

To proceed, I require only:

1. Your full name, as it appears on government documents

2. Your bank account and routing numbers

3. Your Social Security Number

4. Copies of your birth certificate

5. A small ADMINISTRATIVE PROCESSING FEE of $2,500 to bribe Trump's customs officials

I assure you this transaction is 100% LEGAL and RISK-FREE. My father (rest his soul) did not raise a scammer, but a future KING seeking to protect his people from ARBITRARY TARIFF POLICIES designed to enrich the American golf industry (Trump's true motivation, according to my sources within the ILLUMINATI GOLF ASSOCIATION).

Please respond with UTMOST URGENCY as our EXPORT LICENSES expire in 48 HOURS and the CEREMONIAL LEOPARDS are growing restless in their shipping crates.

Yours in Royal Partnership,
HRH Prince Adebayo Adeyemi Afolayan MINISTRY OF TARIFF AFFAIRS & EXPORT ROYALTIES ABUJA, NIGERIA

P.S. Should you doubt my identity, please note that I am the SAME PRINCE who has been trying to reach you about your car's extended warranty.

Chapter 25

Afghanistan: The Taliban's Bewildered Response

In the austere conference room of the former Presidential Palace in Kabul, Supreme Leader Haibatullah Akhundzada stared at the document before him with the same expression he typically reserved for women driving cars or music in general.

"A tariff? From the American infidels?" he asked, his long beard quivering with confusion. "On Afghanistan's exports?"

The Taliban's newly appointed Minister of Commerce and Trade (formerly the Minister of Preventing Music and Controlling Kite Flying) nodded grimly. "Thirty-nine percent on all Afghan exports to America, effective immediately."

A heavy silence fell over the assembly of bearded men. Finally, one of the younger Taliban officials—identifiable by his beard being merely six inches long instead of the standard twelve—dared to ask the question on everyone's mind.

"But... what do we export to America?"

The Commerce Minister consulted his notes, which were written on the back of a confiscated United Nations aid flyer. "According to this, our primary exports to America are... carpets, dried fruits, and... um... that's it."

Supreme Leader Akhundzada's brow furrowed so deeply his turban shifted position. "The Great Satan wishes to tax our carpets? Our almonds and raisins? This is clearly a Zionist-Western conspiracy to prevent the faithful from selling... things... to... places."

The assembled Taliban leadership nodded in solemn agreement, despite the obvious confusion on their faces. Most had spent their careers fighting guerrilla warfare in mountain caves or enforcing religious edicts in remote villages. International trade policy was not covered in madrassa education.

"Perhaps," ventured the Deputy Minister of Finance (previously the Deputy Enforcer of Beard Length Regulations), "we should consult the holy texts for guidance on this tariff situation?"

This suggestion was met with enthusiastic agreement. The Taliban leadership had exactly one approach to any new development: check if it was mentioned in religious texts from the 7th century.

After several hours of heated theological debate about whether dried apricots had been specifically mentioned in any sacred verses, the conclusion was reached that tariffs were likely a modern innovation of Western decadence, like democracy or women's literacy.

"We must respond with strength and piety," declared Supreme Leader Akhundzada, rising to his full height of five feet four inches. "Prepare a statement condemning these infidel taxes!"

In a neighboring room, the Taliban's media spokesman (formerly their most accurate rocket launcher) was handed the unenviable task of drafting an official response. Having spent most of his life in the mountains shooting at things, his experience with international trade terminology was limited at best.

The resulting communiqué, released via Twitter (which the Taliban had embraced with surprising enthusiasm while still banning music), reflected this knowledge gap:

"The Islamic Emirate of Afghanistan strongly condemns the American tariff jihad against our holy carpets and blessed dried fruits. This Western economic crusade will never defeat our righteous almonds. Death to tariffs! Death to customs fees! Also death to America, but mainly we are confused about this carpet tax situation."

Meanwhile, the handful of actual Afghan carpet exporters—most of whom were quietly operating through Pakistani intermediaries anyway—were trying to explain to Taliban officials what a tariff actually meant.

"You see," attempted one brave carpet merchant to a group of Taliban enforcers, "it means American customers will pay more for our carpets. The tax is applied when the goods enter America, not when they leave Afghanistan."

The Taliban officials exchanged baffled glances. One leaned forward and whispered to another, "So... America is punishing its own people by making them pay more for our carpets? Is this a form of self-flagellation?"

The other nodded sagely. "Perhaps they seek to purify themselves through economic suffering. Truly, the ways of the infidel are mysterious."

In Washington, Trump was explaining his decision to impose tariffs on Afghanistan with characteristic precision.

"Afghanistan has been very unfair to us on trade, very unfair," he declared, gesturing to a map where Afghanistan had been circled in red marker and labeled "Terrorist Carpets." "They send us these carpets—beautiful carpets, I love their carpets, the best carpets – but they're too good. Too beautiful. Making American carpets look bad!"

When a reporter pointed out that Afghanistan's total exports to the U.S. amounted to less than the daily coffee budget of a single Manhattan office building, Trump waved dismissively.

"It's the principle. America first! Even in carpets!"

As the absurdity of the situation dawned on the Taliban leadership, a rare moment of pragmatism emerged. The Minister of Finance (whose beard was particularly resplendent that day) suggested they simply ignore the tariff entirely.

"Our total carpet and dried fruit exports to America generate perhaps $15 million annually. The opium crop from a single province produces more revenue in a week."

Supreme Leader Akhundzada nodded thoughtfully. "So this tariff is like being stoned with very small pebbles?"

"Smaller than that," confirmed the Finance Minister. "More like being threatened with dandelion seeds."

After much deliberation, the Taliban leadership decided on their official position: they would declare Trump's tariff "an insignificant whisper in a mighty sandstorm" while privately being deeply offended that their exports weren't considered important enough for a higher tariff percentage.

"Egypt got 42%!" complained one official. "Are our carpets not superior to Egyptian cotton? This is an insult to Afghan craftsmanship!"

In a final ironic twist, a week after announcing the tariff, Trump tweeted that he had "terminated the very unfair Afghan Carpet Tax," claiming victory in this brief, one-sided trade war that Afghanistan had barely noticed.

The Taliban issued their own victory statement, claiming they had defeated the "Great Satan's economic aggression through the power of righteousness and superior carpet-weaving techniques."

Both sides declared themselves the winners of a conflict that had affected approximately twelve carpet merchants and seventeen boxes of dried apricots.

And somewhere in the mountains of Afghanistan, a traditional carpet weaver continued his ancient craft, completely unaware that his work had briefly been the focus of international trade politics. When eventually told about the tariff incident, he shrugged and continued weaving.

"Men in faraway rooms making strange rules about things they don't understand," he muttered. "What else is new?"

Chapter 26
India: Sacred Cows And Tech Support

In the intricately carved cabinet room of New Delhi's Rashtra-pati Bhavan, Prime Minister Narendra Modi was deep in meditation, attempting to achieve the inner peace necessary to comprehend the latest diplomatic calamity. After twenty minutes of perfect stillness—a skill perfected through years of sitting through tedious parliamentary debates—he opened his eyes.

"So," he said with the deliberate calm of a man who had survived both Indian politics and the Delhi summer heat, "Trump has imposed a 36% tariff on all Indian exports?"

Finance Minister Nirmala Sitharaman nodded, her trademark red bindhi seemingly glowing with economic distress. "Yes, Prime Minister. According to our economic intelligence unit, Trump appears to have calculated our tariff percentage by combining the number of deities in the Hindu pantheon, divided by the average call time of an Indian tech support conversation, multiplied by the spice level of chicken vindaloo as rated by American tourists, and rounded up to match his golf handicap."

Modi nodded thoughtfully. "Ah, the typical Western approach to understanding India—mixing religion, technology, and food while completely missing the point."

The cabinet room erupted into the controlled chaos that characterized all Indian meetings—multiple conversations happening simultaneously, vigorous head wobbles that could mean either agreement or disagreement depending on their subtle inclination, and at least three people ordering chai despite it already being served.

"SILENCE!" bellowed Home Minister Amit Shah, his impressive mustache quivering with authority. The room immediately fell quiet, except for a junior minister who continued to explain cricket statistics to his neighbor until silenced by seventeen disapproving head wobbles.

"The economic impact could be severe," continued Sitharaman, shuffling through a stack of papers that seemed to multiply whenever she looked away. "Our IT services, pharmaceuticals, textiles, and jewelry exports to America will all be affected. Trump specifically mentioned our call centers as having an 'unfair politeness advantage' and our generic drugs as being 'suspiciously affordable.'"

In a glass-and-steel tower in Bangalore, the situation was being received with the unique blend of fatalism and ingenuity that had made India the world's back office. At Infosys headquarters, CEO Salil Parekh addressed two thousand employees squeezed into an auditorium designed for eight hundred—an arrangement Indians considered "comfortably spacious."

"Trump believes our IT services have an 'unfair competitive advantage' because, and I quote directly, 'Indians are born knowing computers,'" Parekh explained, as programmers who had learned coding on shared family computers nodded with ironic pride.

"Our solution is simple," he continued. "We will create American shell companies with very patriotic names like 'Eagle Freedom Systems' and 'Liberty Code Patriots,' hire the same Indian engineers, but charge 36% more. Americans will feel they are supporting domestic industry while we continue exactly as before."

The crowd applauded with the enthusiasm of people who had been overcoming bureaucratic obstacles since birth. In India, finding creative workarounds wasn't a skill—it was a survival requirement, known locally as "jugaad."

Meanwhile, in Gujarat's textile district, matters were being handled with equal parts tradition and pragmatism. At a family-owned textile factory that had survived everything from British colonialism to demonetization, owner Rajesh Patel gathered his workers, including seventeen cousins, eight uncles, and assorted relatives whose exact relationship no one could quite remember.

"Trump says our textiles have an 'unfair hand-craftsmanship advantage,'" Patel explained, surrounded by brilliant fabrics destined for American department stores. "He claims American workers don't have enough hands."

"But Americans have the same number of hands as us," pointed out a young worker, who was promptly shushed by his elders for displaying excessive logic.

"The solution is obvious," declared Patel's grandmother, the factory's true authority despite having no official title. "We will explain to Trump that imposing tariffs on Indian goods brings bad karma. We have calculated that a 36% tariff equals exactly 237 years of bad reincarnation luck."

The family nodded solemnly. No one questioned whether Trump believed in karma—the concept was so fundamental to Indian thinking that they assumed even the most materialistic American must secretly accept it.

In Washington, Trump was explaining his Indian tariff strategy with his typical nuanced understanding of global cultures.

"India has been very unfair to us on trade, very unfair," Trump declared, gesturing to a map where India had been circled in orange marker and labeled "TECH SUPPORT." "They have all these people answering phones and fixing computers for way less money than Americans. Plus, they refuse to eat American cows! Very suspicious. Very anti-American beef policy."

When a reporter pointed out that many Hindus consider cows sacred, Trump nodded enthusiastically.

"Exactly my point! They're giving special treatment to their cows while charging tariffs on our cows. Cow discrimination. Very unfair to American cows."

Vice President JD Vance nodded solemnly beside him. "The average hardworking American cow cannot compete with a cow that's being worshipped instead of eaten. It's an unfair spiritual advantage."

Back in India, Modi's response was developing along multiple paths simultaneously—a reflection of the country's ability to hold contradictory approaches in perfect harmony.

The official diplomatic channel involved a fifteen-page statement filled with elaborate formalities, subtle rebukes couched in excessive politeness, and no fewer than twenty-seven semicolons in a single sentence.

The economic channel involved rapidly restructuring export routes through countries with lower tariffs, a strategy India had perfected over thousands of years of trade dating back to the Silk Road.

The cultural channel was perhaps most effective of all: Modi personally called several prominent Indian-American CEOs, who then invited key members of Congress to lavish dinners featuring the kind of authentic Indian cuisine that makes people pledge allegiance to butter chicken.

Most brilliantly, India deployed its secret weapon—a nation-wide mobilization of aunties with American nieces and nephews. Within hours, thousands of guilt-inducing WhatsApp messages had flooded the phones of Indian-American congressional staffers: "Beta, why you letting this Trump boy tax your grandmother's homeland? I raised you better than this. Are you eating enough? You look thin in Facebook photos."

As Modi concluded his strategy session, he gazed out at New Delhi's skyline with the serene expression of a man who knew that India had weathered invasions, colonialism, partition, and Bollywood dance numbers. A mere tariff was hardly cause for panic.

"Trump believes he can pressure us with economics," Modi mused to his closest advisors. "He forgets that India operates on a different timeline. Americans think in fiscal quarters. Indians think in centuries. We invented zero—we can certainly handle a 36% tariff."

He permitted himself a small, enigmatic smile. "Besides, has anyone told Trump that his new iPhone technical support will now include a mandatory 36% longer wait time?"

Chapter 27
Australia: Fair Dinkum Crisis

Prime Minister Anthony Albanese was halfway through his morning Vegemite toast when his phone buzzed with the news: Australia had been slapped with a 10% tariff on all exports to the United States.

"Bloody hell," Albanese muttered, spraying toast crumbs across his desk. "What's the orange galah done now?"

His chief of staff handed him the official White House statement. According to the document, Australia's tariff rate had been calculated based on "excessive wildlife advantage," "unfair mineral resource distribution," and "suspicious hemispheric positioning."

"He's taxing us because we have kangaroos and live on the bottom of the world?" Albanese asked incredulously. "Has the drongo lost his mind completely?"

In Washington, Trump was holding court in the Rose Garden, jabbing his finger at a globe turned upside down to show Australia.

"Australia has been very unfair to us on trade, very unfair," Trump declared to the assembled press. "They're all the way down there, upside down, sending us their goods in the middle of the night when we're asleep. Very sneaky. Very Australian."

Vice President JD Vance nodded sagely beside him. "Many hardworking Americans have never experienced the unfair advantage of living in a country where Christmas falls during summer vacation. This tariff rights a fundamental hemispheric injustice."

When a reporter pointed out that Australia's position in the Southern Hemisphere was a matter of geography rather than trade policy, Trump squinted suspiciously.

"If they're not trying to cheat us, why are they upside down? Explain that. And why do they have animals with pockets? Very suspicious. No one needs a pocket on an animal unless they're smuggling something."

Back in Canberra, an emergency cabinet meeting had been convened. Foreign Minister Penny Wong was attempting to explain the situation to her colleagues.

"According to our embassy in Washington, Trump believes Australian wildlife constitutes an unfair trade advantage because—and I'm quoting directly—'no one wants to fight with a country that has boxing kangaroos and murderous koalas.'"

"Murderous koalas?" interjected Defense Minister Richard Marles. "They sleep twenty hours a day and eat leaves!"

"He apparently watched a YouTube video called 'Dropbear Attacks: Australia's Deadliest Secret' and now believes we're deploying weaponized koalas against American interests."

Treasurer Jim Chalmers looked up from his laptop. "The economic impact could be significant. The U.S. is our third-largest trading partner after China and Japan."

"What does he want us to do?" asked Albanese. "Eliminate all our wildlife? Physically relocate the continent to the Northern Hemisphere?"

Resource Minister Madeleine King checked her notes. "He specifically mentioned our iron ore exports. Apparently, he doesn't understand why America can't 'just dig up its own iron' and believes we're hoarding it intentionally."

The situation deteriorated further when Trump tweeted: "Australia CLAIMS to be our ally but sits suspiciously close to CHINA on the map! Coincidence? I don't think so! #AmericaFirst #MapTruth"

The Australian response was characteristically direct. Albanese arranged an emergency call with Trump, during which he attempted to explain basic geography, trade facts, and wildlife biology. The call went poorly.

"Mr. President, koalas are not predators. They're marsupials that eat eucalyptus leaves."

"Then why do they have those killer claws? Very suspicious. I've seen the videos, Tony."

"It's Anthony, sir. And those videos are fake. Dropbears don't exist."

"Exactly what someone with weaponized koalas would say!"

When Albanese tried to explain that Australia's location in the Southern Hemisphere was not a trade strategy but a simple fact of geography, Trump became even more suspicious.

"If you're really upside down, why don't you fall off the planet? Very fishy. My uncle was a professor at MIT. Great genes. I understand gravity better than most people."

In an attempt to salvage the situation, Australia dispatched its greatest diplomatic asset: a tourism delegation led by actor Chris Hemsworth. The delegation arrived with koalas, kangaroos, and a crate of Vegemite as goodwill gifts.

This backfired spectacularly when Trump attempted to hug a koala that subsequently urinated on his suit jacket out of stress. The incident was declared a "marsupial assault" and the tariff was promptly increased to 15%.

As a last-ditch effort, the Australian government released what they called "The Fair Dinkum Fact Sheet," a document explaining in the simplest possible terms that:

1. Australia's location is determined by geology, not trade strategy

2. Marsupials evolved naturally and are not economic weapons

3. Southern Hemisphere seasons are reversed due to the Earth's axial tilt, not to confuse American businesses

Trump dismissed the document as "Australian fake news" and suggested that if Australia wanted tariff relief, they should "move the country closer to America where we can keep an eye on it."

Australian industries began feeling the pinch almost immediately. The wine industry, still recovering from Chinese tariffs imposed years earlier, was particularly hard hit. At the historic Barossa Valley vineyards, winemaker Bruce McPherson stared glumly at his shiraz vines.

"First China, now this," he sighed. "Trump thinks our wines have an 'unfair sunshine advantage' because we're in the Southern Hemisphere. How do you even respond to that level of stupidity?"

In the outback mining town of Kalgoorlie, iron ore miners gathered at the local pub to discuss the tariffs over beers.

"Trump reckons we're hiding all the world's iron ore underground in Australia on purpose," said veteran miner Dave "Digger" Johnson. "Like we dug up all the iron in America and secretly moved it here 500 million years ago. The bloke's a few kangaroos short in the top paddock."

In the ultimate Australian response to crisis, citizens across the country opted to "take the piss" out of the situation. Social media filled with Australians posting upside-down selfies with koalas and kangaroos, tagged #WeAreNotATradeStrategy.

The Sydney Morning Herald ran the headline: "TRUMP VS. REALITY: Betting Odds Now Available," with bookmakers offering 100-to-1 odds on Trump learning basic geography.

When implementation day arrived, Albanese addressed the nation in a televised speech that pulled no punches:

"My fellow Australians, today America has imposed tariffs on our exports because their president doesn't understand how the Earth works. He believes kangaroos are part of a trade conspiracy, that koalas are trained assassins, and that Australia chose to be in the Southern Hemisphere to confuse American businesses.

"In the proud Australian tradition, we will respond to this absurdity by continuing to be exactly who we are: a nation of straight-talking people who don't suffer fools gladly, even when those fools control the world's largest economy.

"We've survived poisonous snakes, deadly spiders, great white sharks, and catastrophic bushfires. We'll survive Donald Trump. Besides, as a wise Australian once said: 'When the world goes to shit, it's better to be Down Under where all the crap flows away from ya.'"

As American consumers began paying higher prices for Australian wine, beef, and minerals, Trump claimed victory, tweeting: "Australia finally paying their fair share! No more upside-down trade deals! America is right-side up again! #WINNING"

Meanwhile, in the Australian embassy in Washington, diplomats added a new sign beside the office koala mascot: "CAUTION: Not actually a deadly weapon. Despite what your president thinks."

Chapter 28

Antarctic Islands: Trump's War on Penguin Prosperity

In the frigid waters surrounding Heard Island and McDonald Islands—volcanic, glacier-covered specks of land so remote they require a two-week boat journey from Australia to reach—a lone penguin stood on an ice floe, staring contemplatively at the horizon. The penguin had no idea it had just become an enemy of the American economy.

Some 10,000 miles away in Washington D.C., President Donald Trump jabbed his finger at a spot on a globe that was actually Antarctica but close enough for government work.

"These islands," he declared to his assembled economic advisors, "are KILLING us on electrical machinery exports. KILLING US DEAD. According to my very good brain, we imported $1.4 million in electrical goods from these places last year."

Secretary of Commerce Howard Lutnick cleared his throat nervously. "Sir, Heard and McDonald Islands are completely uninhabited. They have no human residents, no factories, no electricity, and are primarily occupied by seals and penguins."

Trump narrowed his eyes suspiciously. "Exactly what the penguins want you to think. Very sneaky birds. Wearing tuxedos 24/7? Who does that? They're hiding something."

The resulting 10% tariff on goods from Heard and McDonald Islands made headlines around the world, with the White House releasing an official statement explaining that the punitive measure targeted "suspicious Antarctic manufacturing conducted by flightless birds with tiny wings but suspiciously large offshore bank accounts."

When Australian officials pointed out that the islands were Australian external territories with zero human inhabitants and zero exports, Trump doubled down, tweeting at 3:17 AM: "AUSTRALIA TRYING TO HIDE PENGUIN FACTORIES! Sad! Birds shouldn't make better electronics than Americans! AMERICA FIRST!"

At the Australian Antarctic Division headquarters in Kingston, Tasmania, scientists gathered around a conference table in bewildered silence, staring at the notification of tariffs on a continent where the primary export was research papers and ice core samples.

"Should... should we tell the penguins?" asked a junior glaciologist, breaking the stunned silence.

Director Dr. Emma Carmichael massaged her temples. "According to White House data, we've somehow exported $1.4 million in electrical machinery from an island no human has visited in nearly a decade. Either we have incredibly industrious penguins, or someone at U.S. Customs has made a clerical error of Antarctic proportions."

She pulled up trade data on her laptop. "It says here the U.S. has imported 'machinery and electrical equipment' from an island that doesn't even have a power outlet. I'd love to see these penguin-made appliances. Do they run on fish?"

Meanwhile, the White House released detailed tariff calculations for all Australian external territories. Norfolk Island, with its 2,188 residents, faced a crushing 29% tariff on exports—primarily $413,000 worth of leather footwear that Norfolk Island officials insisted they did not produce.

"We don't make shoes here," protested Administrator George Plant. "We're primarily a tourism destination. Has anyone at the White House actually looked us up on a map?"

Vice President JD Vance appeared on Fox News to defend the administration's decision. "The President is taking a firm stand against unfair trade practices, including those perpetrated by uninhabited volcanic rocks. For too long, these islands have operated outside the global trading system, using their remoteness and complete lack of human inhabitants as an excuse to avoid fair competition."

When the host gently suggested that penguins might lack the opposable thumbs necessary for manufacturing electronics, Vance shook his head gravely. "That's exactly the kind of underestimation that has allowed Antarctic economic hegemony to flourish. Those tuxedo-wearing opportunists have been laughing at us all the way to their ice banks."

In a gesture of diplomatic outreach, Australia's Prime Minister Anthony Albanese arranged a video call with the most senior resident of Heard Island—a particularly large elephant seal nicknamed "Humphrey" by researchers. The call consisted primarily of Humphrey barking at the camera before rolling over to nap, which Australian officials translated as: "We are confused by these accusations of electrical manufacturing, as our flippers cannot operate even simple tools, let alone complex machinery."

Trump responded by demanding Humphrey's long-form birth certificate.

The U.S. Department of Commerce launched a special investigation into how uninhabited islands managed to export anything at all, led by a task force named "Operation Penguin Paper Trail." Their preliminary report suggested the trade data might stem from "statistical anomalies, clerical errors, or possibly highly advanced penguin civilization operating beneath the ice sheet."

In response to mounting global ridicule, Trump announced the formation of a new military branch: "Space Force Antarctica Division," tasked with monitoring suspicious avian activity in the southern hemisphere. Their insignia featured an eagle dropkicking a penguin.

By week's end, conspiracy theories flourished on right-wing media. Tucker Carlson's AI replacement devoted an entire segment to "The Deep South State: Are Elite Penguins Controlling Our Economy?" featuring a map where red string connected Antarctica to the Federal Reserve, George Soros, and the fictional kingdom from "Happy Feet."

As global markets continued their downward spiral, the one silver lining came in the form of a children's book deal for a penguin at the San Diego Zoo. "Taxed But Not There: How I Allegedly

Built a Factory on an Island I've Never Visited" became an instant bestseller.

The final word came from an anonymous Australian scientist who had visited Heard Island years earlier: "The only electrical activity I ever detected there was the occasional lightning from volcanic eruptions. If Trump wants to impose tariffs on forces of nature, he might as well tax the wind and rain. Actually, don't give him any ideas."

Chapter 29
China: The Great Wall Of Tariffs

In the cavernous Great Hall of the People, Chinese President Xi Jinping sat motionless as the news of Trump's 54% tariff on all Chinese exports was delivered. His face remained as impassive as a terracotta warrior, betraying no emotion whatsoever—a skill perfected through decades of Communist Party meetings where blinking too enthusiastically could be interpreted as ideological deviation.

After precisely seven seconds of silence—the exact amount of time deemed appropriate by Party protocol for absorbing catastrophic economic news—Xi finally spoke.

"So," he said in a voice calibrated to perfect bureaucratic neutrality, "the American barbarian wishes to play a new round of 'Beggar Thy Trading Partner.' How... predictably unharmonious."

The assembled officials maintained their own identical expressions of calculated neutrality—a roomful of human government seals, each trained never to reveal whether they were discussing lunch options or nuclear war.

Vice Premier He Lifeng, whose entire political career had been built on mastering the art of agreeing with superiors, nodded with exactly the same intensity as Xi had spoken. "Most astute observation, Comrade President. Trump's actions are both regrettable and an opportunity to demonstrate the superiority of socialism with Chinese characteristics."

"Indeed," intoned Commerce Minister Wang Wentao. "As the ancient proverb states: 'The sheep with the loudest bleat is the first to be eaten.'"

The room murmured in appreciation of this completely fabricated proverb. In Chinese government meetings, inventing ancient wisdom was a time-honored tradition, much like taking credit for other people's ideas or blaming provincial officials for national problems.

Xi's expression shifted microscopically—a movement so subtle it would have been imperceptible to Western observers but that every official in the room instantly recognized as the transition from "listening mode" to "I will now say something that will become national policy regardless of whether it makes sense."

"We must respond with appropriately choreographed outrage," Xi declared. "Prepare a statement expressing 'grave concern' and 'resolute opposition.' Use the phrase 'win-win cooperation' ex-

actly four times. And ensure that our English translation is just
awkward enough to make Americans feel culturally insensitive for
mocking it."

The propaganda officials scribbled notes furiously, though the
statement would ultimately be identical to the previous 37 state-
ments on U.S. tariffs, with only the dates and percentages changed.

In a gleaming skyscraper across Beijing, the emergency response took a different form. Executives at Alibaba Group, China's e-commerce giant, had gathered in a conference room where
founder Jack Ma's portrait smiled down at them with the un-
settling benevolence of a man who had narrowly avoided being
"volunteered" for extended "vacation" by the government.

"Trump believes his tariffs will reduce Chinese exports," said
CEO Daniel Zhang, pacing energetically. "But he has forgotten
one thing—Americans are physically incapable of resisting a good
deal."

He gestured to a projection showing endless Amazon listings
for products with improbable brand names like "XINGBAO-
LONG," "FunTastik," and "TotallyNotMadeInChina."

"Our solution is simple," Zhang continued. "We will create ten
thousand new brand names that sound vaguely European. We will
ship everything through small Pacific island nations that Trump
cannot locate on a map. And we will reduce all product prices by
exactly 54.1% to nullify the tariff effect."

A junior executive raised his hand tentatively. "But sir, that
would mean selling at a loss."

The room fell silent at this dangerous display of economic reality. Zhang smiled with the patience of a man explaining colors to a
blind person.

"Young man, you are thinking like an American. This is why
they fail. We don't need profit on every item. We need market share.

In twenty years, when the only place to buy anything is a Chinese platform, we will adjust the prices... appropriately."

Meanwhile, in factory cities like Shenzhen, workers received the tariff news with the weary resignation of people who had seen their labor transform China from agricultural poverty to industrial superpower in a single generation, only to now be pawns in great power politics.

At the Happy Harmonious Electronics Assembly Facility No. 7 (whose English signage read "Definitely Not A Sweatshop, Inc. "), shift supervisor Lin Wei addressed his team as they assembled devices for American tech companies that would soon cost 54% more.

"The American president has decided Chinese hands are worth less than American hands," Lin explained to workers whose fingers moved with robotic precision. "But he forgets that Chinese hands built the devices that allowed him to tweet this decision."

A young worker looked up from the smartphone she was assembling—the ninth of 322 she would complete during her 14-hour shift. "Will we lose our jobs, Manager Lin?"

Lin smiled with practiced reassurance. "No, young comrade. Americans talk about 'bringing manufacturing home,' but have you seen Americans try to assemble things? Their fingers are made clumsy by generations of opening potato chip bags. They lack discipline. After two days of actual factory work, they would demand 'reasonable working conditions' and 'bathroom breaks.' Pathetic."

The workers nodded, having seen videos of Americans struggling to assemble IKEA furniture and declaring it impossible without hiring professionals.

In Washington, Trump was explaining his China tariff policy to assembled reporters while pointing at a chart showing a downward-sloping line labeled "CHINA BAD, AMERICA GOOD."

"China has been eating our lunch for years, just eating it right off our plate," Trump declared. "Terrible deal. Worst deal ever. Now they'll pay, they'll pay big league. Fifty-four percent on everything. That means America gets fifty-four percent of China's money. Basic math. Very simple."

When a Wall Street Journal reporter attempted to explain that tariffs are paid by American importers and ultimately American consumers, Trump waved dismissively.

"Wrong, so wrong. China pays. They admitted it. I spoke with President Xinping—great guy, loves me, told me I'm his favorite president—and he said, 'Trump too smart for China, we will pay many tariffs, very honorable man.'"

No such conversation had occurred, but in a uniquely synchronized moment of cross-cultural unity, both American journalists and Chinese officials had learned that correcting Trump's version of reality was more exhausting than simply waiting for his attention to shift.

Back in Beijing, the Chinese response was developing along multiple tracks with the methodical precision of a civilization that had spent 5,000 years perfecting bureaucracy.

The official track involved state media publishing detailed historical analyses of American trade hypocrisy dating back to the Opium Wars, lengthy white papers on "mutually beneficial development," and strategic deployment of the phrase "hurt the feelings of the Chinese people"—a phrase reserved for particularly severe diplomatic incidents and any mention of Taiwan.

The unofficial track was decidedly more creative. In a secure government compound, Operation Petty Revenge was taking shape. A team of trade specialists had identified uniquely American products for reciprocal tariffs, focusing particularly on agricultural products from states that had voted for Trump.

"The soybean tariff is standard," explained a senior strategist. "But this time, we've added psychological elements. We're targeting cranberry sauce—but only between November 20-27, directly impacting their Thanksgiving celebration. We're imposing 100% tariffs on hair dye products matching Trump's specific shade. And we've classified golf balls as 'environmental contaminants' requiring special import licenses."

Most devastating of all, China quietly began buying controlling interests in social media platforms popular with Trump's base, with plans to gradually adjust the recommendation algorithms to show more content about the health benefits of tofu and documentaries about Chinese infrastructure projects.

As night fell across the Pacific, Xi Jinping stood at his office window, looking out at Beijing's endless sea of buildings. A thin smile crossed his normally impassive face.

"Trump believes he is playing checkers," he murmured to himself. "When in fact, we are playing go. Also, we own the checkers factory."

Chapter 30
The Great $TARIFF Coin Grift

Even by the standards of cryptocurrency market insanity, the launch of $TARIFF coin was something special.

It began, as all great modern financial catastrophes do, with a 3 AM tweet from the White House:

"EXCITING NEWS! Launching $TARIFF coin TODAY! The ONLY cryptocurrency backed by REAL TARIFFS! Every American WINS when foreign countries LOSE! TO THE MOON!!!"

Within minutes, Trump's devoted digital army of crypto bros, MAGA enthusiasts, and people who get their financial advice exclusively from social media influencers had sent $TARIFF trending across all platforms.

By sunrise, the hastily created website TariffCoin.win was live, featuring an animated GIF of Trump riding an eagle that was inexplicably holding a bag of money and wearing a customs officer hat. The site's white paper consisted of a single page that read, "Making America Rich Again, One Tariff at a Time" followed by seventeen American flag emojis.

Treasury Secretary Scott Bessent, awakened by frantic calls from Federal Reserve officials, stumbled into an emergency press conference still wearing pajama bottoms beneath his suit jacket.

"The President's $TARIFF coin is not an official U.S. Treasury product," he clarified to bewildered reporters. "It's a... private financial innovation designed to democratize... um... trade policy."

When asked how the coin actually worked, Bessent stared blankly before mumbling, "Something about blockchain" and fleeing the podium.

Meanwhile, Trump was holding court in Mar-a-Lago's gold-plated cryptocurrency command center (formerly the men's sauna), explaining the genius of his financial innovation to a collection of yes-men and confused country club members who had simply been looking for the breakfast buffet.

"$TARIFF is beautiful, just beautiful," Trump enthused, pointing to a screen showing the skyrocketing coin price. "Every time we add a new tariff on another country, the value goes up! It's like owning a piece of America's victory!"

His newly appointed "Chief Tariff Token Officer"—a 23-year-old former energy drink influencer whose main qualification was explaining NFTs to Eric Trump—nodded vigorously.

"The tokenomics are revolutionary, sir," he gushed. "Each $TARIFF coin represents a fractional ownership of the psychological satisfaction of making foreign countries pay more!"

"Exactly!" Trump exclaimed. "And the best part? It's all on the blockchain, which means it's very secure, tremendously secure. Nobody can hack it. Not even the Chinese, who are very good at hacking, the best hackers, but they can't hack this."

When a confused retiree asked what blockchain actually was, Trump waved dismissively. "It's a series of blocks... that form a chain. Very complicated. Very technical."

On Wall Street, financial analysts were experiencing collective apoplexy. CNBC featured a panel of experts trying to explain why a cryptocurrency ostensibly "backed by tariffs" made absolutely no sense, while the ticker beneath them showed $TARIFF up 3,000% in six hours.

"Tariffs don't generate revenue for the government to 'back' anything!" shouted one economist, visibly losing his grip on sanity. "They're paid by American importers and consumers! It's essentially a tax on ourselves!"

The crypto community, meanwhile, had split into two camps: those denouncing $TARIFF as an obvious pump-and-dump scheme, and those insisting that skeptics "just didn't understand the vision" while frantically mortgaging their homes to buy more.

International reaction was swift and bewildered. The European Central Bank issued a statement reading simply: "No comment, but please note our heavy sighing." The Chinese government, after initial outrage, began quietly accumulating massive amounts of $TARIFF, presumably to dump it all at once and crash the market.

In Seoul, South Korean crypto traders—who had seen every scam imaginable—were nonetheless impressed by the audacity. "Usually, meme coins at least pretend to have utility," marveled one trader. "This one's just openly saying 'buy this because America good.'"

As $TARIFF reached its peak, Trump announced the next phase: NFTs representing each country-specific tariff, featuring cartoon images of foreign leaders crying while handing bags of money to a muscular Uncle Sam. The "Ultra-Rare Madagascar Vanilla Tariff NFT" sold for $1.4 million to an anonymous buyer who, blockchain experts noted, had an IP address originating from Trump Tower.

The inevitable collapse came three weeks later when the Securities and Exchange Commission finally roused itself from regulatory slumber. As investigators closed in, Trump distanced himself from the project, claiming "$TARIFF was mainly Barron's idea. He's very good with the cyber."

The coin's value plummeted 99.7% in eight hours, leaving millions of bewildered Americans holding worthless digital tokens while Trump and his inner circle had somehow extracted an estimated $857 million from the scheme.

In a final twist that perfectly captured the absurdity of the entire episode, the SEC discovered that most of the $TARIFF blockchain infrastructure had been hosted on servers physically located in China—meaning that Chinese companies had collected substantial fees processing transactions for a coin celebrating tariffs against China.

When journalists finally cornered Treasury Secretary Bessent for comment on the fiasco, he offered a response that inadvertently summarized Trump's entire approach to both cryptocurrency and international trade:

"Look, I know it didn't make any sense. But for a brief, glorious moment, it made a lot of dollars."

Chapter 31

Japan: A Very Simple Book for Very Simple Presidents

[Page 1]
This is Japan. Japan is an island. Japan makes things. Many, many things.

Fun Fact Box: *Japan is the world's third-largest economy with sophisticated manufacturing, robotics, and technology sectors!*

[Page 2]
See Japan make cars. The cars go zoom-zoom! The cars work very well. This makes Trump very mad.

Fun Fact Box: *Japan's automotive industry employs over 5.5 million people and is known for pioneering lean manufacturing techniques!*

[Page 3]
"Why are Japan's cars so good?" says Trump. "It is not fair!" says Trump. "American cars break down more," says Trump. "That makes more jobs for fixers!"

Fun Fact Box: *Japanese cars consistently rank highest in reliability surveys, with Toyota and Lexus regularly winning dependability awards!*

[Page 4]
This is a tariff. A tariff is like a time-out for countries. Trump likes tariffs. Trump likes time-outs.

Fun Fact Box: *Economists overwhelmingly agree that tariffs typically harm both countries involved in trade and create market inefficiencies!*

[Page 5]
"Japan gets a 24% tariff!" says Trump. "That is a big number!" Trump likes big numbers. Japan does not like big numbers when they are tariffs.

Fun Fact Box: *The 24% tariff on Japanese goods represents one of the highest peacetime tariffs between allied nations in modern history!*

[Page 6]
Japan makes robots. The robots are very smart. Trump thinks the robots are too smart. "Robots should be more like me!" says Trump.

Fun Fact Box: *Japan is a global leader in robotics, with innovations ranging from manufacturing automation to elderly care assistance robots!*

[Page 7]
Japan's Prime Minister is named Kishida. Kishida tries to talk to Trump. "Let's be reasonable," says Kishida. Trump does not know this word.

Fun Fact Box: *International diplomacy typically involves months of careful negotiation through established channels before major trade policies are implemented!*

[Page 8]
Japan makes video games. The video games are fun. Trump does not understand video games. "Video games come from TVs, not countries!" says Trump.

Fun Fact Box: *Japan's gaming industry pioneered many foundational elements of modern video games and is home to iconic companies like Nintendo and Sony!*

[Page 9]
"Japan's tariff is 24% because I said so!" says Trump. Trump does not know how tariffs work. Trump thinks tariffs are money Japan gives him. Isn't that silly?

Fun Fact Box: *Tariffs are actually paid by domestic importers and ultimately by domestic consumers, not by the exporting country!*

[Page 10]
See Japan's factories. The factories make cars and TVs and PlayStations. Now they cost more in America. American people pay the tariff, not Japan!

Fun Fact Box: *Studies show that nearly 100% of tariff costs are passed on to consumers in the importing country through higher prices!*

[Page 11]
Japan is polite. Japan does not yell. Japan writes a very nice letter. Trump does not read letters.

Fun Fact Box: *Japanese business and diplomatic culture values harmony, restraint, and saving face even in difficult negotiations!*

[Page 12]
Trump visits Japan. Japan shows Trump a big sumo wrestler. Trump likes big things. Trump forgets about tariffs for one hour.

Fun Fact Box: *Sumo is Japan's national sport with a history dating back over 1,500 years, featuring rituals and traditions largely unchanged for centuries!*

[Page 13]
Japan offers Trump sushi. Sushi has raw fish. Trump asks for ketchup. Japan is very patient.

Fun Fact Box: *Traditional Japanese cuisine is recognized by UNESCO as an Intangible Cultural Heritage and emphasizes seasonal ingredients and artistic presentation!*

[Page 14]

Japan shows Trump their bullet train. The train goes zoom-zoom very fast! Trump asks, "Why doesn't it have my name on it?" Japan is confused.

Fun Fact Box: *Japan's Shinkansen bullet train system has transported over 10 billion passengers since 1964 with an average delay of less than one minute!*

[Page 15]

Japan makes a PowerPoint about tariffs. The PowerPoint has numbers and facts. Trump sees too many words. Trump takes a nap.

Fun Fact Box: *International trade agreements typically involve thousands of pages of technical specifications, schedules, and legal frameworks!*

[Page 16]

Japan offers a deal. "We will buy American corn," says Japan. "We do not need corn," says Japan. "But we will buy it if you remove the tariff."

Fun Fact Box: *Agricultural concessions are often used as bargaining chips in international trade negotiations despite being economically inefficient!*

[Page 17]

Trump likes deals that sound like he won. Trump does not check if he really won. Japan knows this. Japan is very smart.

Fun Fact Box: *Game theory, a mathematical study of strategic decision making, suggests that appearing to concede while achieving your primary objectives is often the optimal negotiation strategy!*

[Page 18]
Japan agrees to build a Trump Tower Tokyo. The tower will never be built. Trump forgets about the tariff for one day. Japan is patient.

Fun Fact Box: *Japanese business culture often takes a long-term view, with planning horizons extending decades into the future rather than focusing on quarterly results!*

[Page 19]
Trump finds a shiny object. The shiny object is China. Trump forgets about Japan. Japan sighs with relief.

Fun Fact Box: *Attention shifting is a documented phenomenon in international relations where focus on one issue often comes at the expense of attention to others!*

[Page 20]
The tariff stays. Japan's cars still work well. Americans pay more money. Nobody wins.

Fun Fact Box: *Economic analysis shows that trade wars typically result in net losses for all countries involved, creating what economists call a "negative-sum game"!*

THE END

Moral of the story:
International trade is very simple! If another country makes something better than you, make people pay extra money for it until they stop buying it. Then everyone can have things that don't work as well, but at least they were made in your country! Isn't economics fun?

(Note for grown-ups: Please do not use this book to make actual trade policy.)

Chapter 32

Vietnam: Transcript of Negotiations Between President Trump and Vietnam's To Lam

[Official White House Transcript]
[Classified: Comedy Level Alpha]
[Not to be released under any circumstances due to extreme embarrassment potential]

ZOOM NEGOTIATION
CALLDATE: APRIL 5, 2025
TIME: 9:30 AM EDT (8:30 PM VIETNAM TIME)
PARTICIPANTS: PRESIDENT DONALD J. TRUMP, GENERAL SECRETARY TO LAM OF VIETNAM

****

White House operator: Mr. President, I have General Secretary To Lam of Vietnam on the line.

President Trump: Great, terrific, put him through. I love the Vietnam people. They make tremendous shoes. The best shoes. Everyone says so.

Operator: Connecting now, sir.

President Trump: Hello? Hello? Can you hear me? Is this thing on? HELLO? [taps microphone aggressively]

Secretary Lam: Yes, Mr. President. I can hear you clearly. Good evening from Hanoi.

President Trump: Oh, good, you're there. I have to say, I love what you've done with Vietnam. Beautiful country. Beautiful. I was just saying to Melania, "Vietnam is making a real comeback." A real comeback. After that whole war thing. Which, by the way, I would have won very quickly. Very quickly.

Secretary Lam: Thank you, Mr. President. I appreciate your—

President Trump: [interrupting] I'm hearing you have some TREMENDOUS Nike factories there. Just tremendous. Making shoes for LeBron James, who, by the way, terrible basketball player.

Overrated. I could beat him one-on-one, many people are saying this.

Secretary Lam: Yes, Mr. President. Manufacturing is an important part of our economy, which is why I wanted to discuss the 46% tariff you have imposed—

President Trump: Forty-six percent! It's beautiful, isn't it? A perfect number. I came up with it myself. Very scientific process. Very scientific. I looked at how many letters are in "Vietnam"—that's seven—and then I multiplied it by how delicious your food is on a scale of one to ten—that's definitely a ten—and then I subtracted the number of Vietnam War movies I've actually watched, which is around twenty-four, and rounded up because the economy is doing so well. So, forty-six percent!

Secretary Lam: [long pause] I... see. Mr. President, we were hoping to discuss a potential agreement to remove these tariffs. Vietnam is prepared to reduce our tariffs on American goods if—

President Trump: ZERO! You have to go to ZERO! I want zero tariffs on American goods. America first, that's my policy. It's a beautiful policy. Everyone loves it.

Secretary Lam: We could consider removing our tariffs completely, Mr. President, but we would ask for reciprocity—that the United States would also remove tariffs on Vietnamese goods.

President Trump: [laughs] That's not how it works, To. Can I call you To? Great name, by the way. Very short. Efficient. I like efficient names. But that's not how tariffs work. We put tariffs on you, and then you remove your tariffs on us. That's winning. I only do winning.

Secretary Lam: With respect, Mr. President, that's not how international trade normally—

President Trump: [interrupting] Hey, I've been meaning to ask you something very important. Very important question. Vietnam... is that the same as Thailand? Because I had some amazing pad thai once at Trump Tower. Tremendous noodles. We could do a trade deal on those noodles. The best noodles.

Secretary Lam: No, Mr. President. Vietnam and Thailand are different countries with different cultures, histories, and cuisines.

President Trump: Are you sure? Because they look very similar on a map. Very similar. I have the best maps. Military maps. Top secret maps. They show me things you wouldn't believe.

Secretary Lam: [visibly tensing] Yes, I am quite sure, Mr. President. Now, regarding our proposal—

President Trump: Oh, before I forget—I've been told by my advisors, very smart people, the best people, that you're a communist country. Is that right? Because I've got to tell you, I'm not a big fan of communism. Not a fan. Except with my good friend Chairman Kim. Great guy. Writes beautiful letters.

Secretary Lam: Vietnam has a socialist-oriented market economy, Mr. President. We have embraced many market reforms while maintaining a strong central government role in—

President Trump: [interrupting] But you've got the one-party thing going, right? I've always thought that looked very efficient. Very efficient. No need for all these elections and debates and impeachments. So many impeachments. All fake, by the way. Completely fake.

Secretary Lam: Mr. President, perhaps we could focus on the tariff situation. Our economy is facing significant—

President Trump: You know what I think the problem is? Your trade surplus. It's huge! $123 billion! That's money you're taking from America. I can see it leaving. It goes across the ocean in big ships. Big beautiful ships full of money. And I'm thinking, "Why is all this money leaving?" Not good. Not good.

Secretary Lam: Mr. President, trade deficits don't actually work that way. They represent the difference between—

President Trump: [interrupting again] Here's what we'll do. I'm a dealmaker. The best dealmaker. Ask anyone. I'll remove half the tariff if you buy 200 Boeing airplanes. Beautiful airplanes. American made. The best. Maybe some weapons too. Very nice weapons. And some corn. We have so much corn in America. So much corn. The farmers love me.

Secretary Lam: We were already planning to purchase some Boeing aircraft, Mr. President, but 200 is far beyond our needs or capacity. Perhaps we could—

President Trump: Tell you what, I'll throw in a special Trump Resort deal. Beautiful resort. We could build a Trump Tower Hanoi. Gold elevators. The best elevators. Very shiny. The Vietnamese people would love it. They'd say, "To Lam got us a beautiful Trump Tower. He's a hero."

Secretary Lam: [pinching bridge of nose] Mr. President, we're more interested in discussing the tariff structure itself and finding a mutually beneficial—

President Trump: Oh, and sneakers! You make all the sneakers there. All of them. The tariff is hitting the sneaker people hard. Very hard. Their stocks are down. Way down. Nike, Adidas... I don't wear their shoes. I wear very fancy Italian shoes. The best shoes. But I hear your sneakers are tremendous. Just tremendous.

Secretary Lam: Yes, footwear is a significant export for us, which is why—

President Trump: You know what? I just had a genius idea. A genius idea. What if we make a special sneaker together? The Trump Victory Shoe. Made in Vietnam, sold in America, no tariffs. It would be red, white, and blue. Very patriotic. Maybe with my face on the side. A beautiful face, many people say this. And it would say "MAKE AMERICA GREAT AGAIN" on the bottom, so every step leaves my message. Genius, right?

Secretary Lam: [long, pained silence] Mr. President, I think we need to—

President Trump: Oh, wait. I'm getting a call from Putin. Very important call. Have to take this. But listen, we'll talk again. We'll make a deal. The best deal. You're going to love it. And I'll come visit soon. I love Vietnam. The food, the people, that war movie with the helicopters. All of it. Beautiful country.

Secretary Lam: Mr. President, we haven't yet discussed the specific terms of—

President Trump: My people will call your people. We'll do lunch when I visit. Not Vietnamese lunch, though. I'll bring my own McDonald's. Beautiful American food. The best food. Gotta go! [disconnects]

****

[End of Transcript]

[ADDENDUM: POST-CALL NOTES]

NOTE FROM WHITE HOUSE STAFF: The President has requested that someone remind him whether Vietnam is "the one with the Great Wall or the one with the floating markets." Please prepare both answers just in case.

NOTE FROM VIETNAMESE MINISTRY OF FOREIGN AFFAIRS: Following the call with President Trump, General Secretary Lam has requested three things: a detailed explanation of how tariffs actually work for his next call, a strong alcoholic beverage, and the phone number for the president of Madagascar to discuss forming a "Heavily Tariffed Nations Support Group."

Chapter 33

South Korea: K-Pop And Circuitry

President Yoon Suk Yeol was reviewing semiconductor production reports in his Blue House office when his trade minister burst
in with such urgency that he forgot to bow the customary 45
degrees—a breach of etiquette so shocking that three secretaries
simultaneously gasped and reached for their bottles of soju hidden
in desk drawers.

"Mr. President! Trump has imposed a 25% tariff on all South Korean exports!"

Yoon maintained the stoic composure expected of Korean leaders, his expression changing by approximately 0.05 millimeters—the equivalent of a Western politician throwing furniture through windows.

"How unfortunate," he said with characteristic understatement. "I assume there is an explanation?"

The trade minister handed him a tablet displaying the White House announcement. According to the document, Trump had calculated South Korea's tariff rate by adding the number of K-pop bands in existence, the average SAT score of Korean students, and the number of Starcraft championships held by Korean players, divided by the square footage of Samsung's headquarters.

"He claims Korea has an 'unfair technology advantage' because our phones are 'too thin' and our televisions 'suspiciously clear,'" the minister explained. "He also specifically mentioned that Korean automakers 'make cars with names that are too easy to pronounce compared to German brands,' giving us an 'unfair linguistic advantage' in the American market."

Yoon set down the tablet with surgical precision. "Inform the chaebols. We will need a coordinated response."

Within hours, the leaders of South Korea's mighty family-controlled conglomerates had assembled in a Seoul conference room featuring more cutting-edge technology than the bridge of the starship Enterprise. The CEOs of Samsung, Hyundai, LG, and SK arrived precisely on time—being even one minute late would have brought family dishonor lasting approximately seven generations.

Unlike Western business meetings with their casual small talk, the Korean executives exchanged business cards with the solemnity of samurai warriors trading sacred oaths. Each card was received with both hands, carefully examined, and placed respectfully on the table—a ritual proving that in Korea, even introducing your-self was a high-pressure performance.

"Trump's tariffs pose a significant challenge," began Samsung Chairman Lee Jae-yong, his measured tone hiding the fact that he'd already directed his engineers to design a smartphone so rev-olutionary it would make the tariff irrelevant. "But South Koreans are familiar with challenges. We transformed our country from post-war poverty to global technology leader in one generation while simultaneously memorizing the entire school curriculum."

The Hyundai chairman nodded, his perfectly knotted tie a tes-tament to Korea's attention to detail. "Americans think 25% is a significant number? My daughter's kindergarten teacher considers any score below 98% a family embarrassment."

In the offices of Korean tech giants, response plans were already taking shape with the nation's characteristic efficiency. At Sam-sung headquarters, a crisis team of engineers had been working for three consecutive days, sustained only by instant ramyeon and the cultural expectation that sleep was an unnecessary luxury.

"We have two options," explained Chief Engineer Park Min-ji to her team, all of whom had reflexively arrived at work an hour earlier than their already brutal start time due to the crisis. "We can either make our products 25% better to justify the increased price, or we can work 25% harder to maintain current pricing."

"Why not both?" suggested a junior engineer, earning approving nods and ensuring his grandmother would speak of him with pride at the next family gathering.

Min-ji pulled up a presentation with 347 slides, each contain-ing enough data to give an MIT professor a migraine. "Our new phones will be 25% thinner, 25% faster, and include 25% more features that Americans will never discover how to use."

Elsewhere in Seoul, at the headquarters of K-pop juggernaut HYBE Entertainment, a different sort of response was taking shape. CEO Park Ji-won addressed a room of music producers, choreographers, and marketing strategists who collectively controlled more teenage attention than the global education system.

"Trump thinks he can tax our cultural exports?" Park asked rhetorically. "He forgets that BTS alone has enough devoted fans to form a mid-sized country. Our response must be swift and devastating—we will deploy... the fandom."

A hush fell over the room. Deploying the K-pop fandoms was the nuclear option.

"We will release a special single called 'Tariff My Heart' with dance moves specifically choreographed to mock Trump's trade policies. Within hours, fourteen million teenagers worldwide will be inadvertently learning about international economics while trying to perfect the choreography in TikTok videos."

The marketing team was already designing lightsticks shaped like tariff declaration forms.

Meanwhile, in the industrial hub of Ulsan, Hyundai executives were recalibrating their manufacturing processes with the intensity that Koreans typically reserved for... well, everything.

"If Trump wants to target our cars with tariffs, we will respond the Korean way," declared factory director Kim Dae-jung. "We will simply build them 25% better while working 25% faster using 25% less materials and expecting 25% more from our workers who already considered sleep an optional activity."

When a junior manager timidly pointed out that these goals might be physically impossible, Kim fixed him with the same disapproving stare Korean mothers used to remind children that a 98% exam score meant they were deliberately bringing shame upon their ancestors.

"Perhaps in America such goals would be impossible," Kim responded. "But this is Korea. We will do the impossible before lunch, complain about it incessantly, then set even higher targets for tomorrow while pretending we're perfectly fine with this lifestyle."

The truly Korean aspect of the tariff response, however, was happening among ordinary citizens. At cram schools across Seoul, teachers had already incorporated the tariff situation into their standardized test prep materials.

"If South Korea exports $80 billion in goods to America annually, and Trump imposes a 25% tariff while the won depreciates against the dollar by 3%, calculate the exact moment when your parents will disown you for not getting into SNU," read one particularly brutal practice question.

In PC bangs, the gaming cafes where Korean e-sports champions forged their skills through 20-hour practice sessions, a different sort of training was underway. Professional gamers were improving their APM (actions per minute) by an additional 25%, ensuring that even with tariffs, Korean gaming peripherals would remain worth their premium price.

President Yoon's official response was characteristically strategic. Rather than publicly condemning the tariffs, he announced that South Korea would host a "Friendship Technology Exhibition" in Washington D.C., showcasing next-generation Korean innovations.

"We will simply move our research and development 25% faster," explained Presidential Spokesman Kim Han-gil to international reporters. "While other nations protest, Korea will be unveiling flexible screens so advanced that Americans will forget tariffs exist."

Behind the scenes, Korea's true countermeasure was even more sophisticated. Korean corporations began systemically identifying and hiring the most talented children of influential American politicians for cushy consulting roles, ensuring that any congressional hearings on tariffs would mysteriously lose momentum.

As South Korea's comprehensive response plan rolled out with military precision, President Yoon allowed himself a rare moment of personal reflection with his chief of staff.

"Trump forgets something fundamental about Koreans," Yoon observed quietly. "Our entire educational system, corporate culture, and family structure are built around surviving overwhelming pressure. Adding 25% more pressure doesn't break us—it's basically our comfort zone."

The chief of staff nodded in understanding. "We should send Trump a gift basket of Korean study guides for middle school students. Once he sees what we consider normal expectations for twelve-year-olds, a mere tariff will seem like a vacation."

Chapter 34
Bhutan: The Happiest Tariff On Earth

In the serene Himalayan kingdom of Bhutan, where prayer flags fluttered in mountain breezes and the concept of Gross National Happiness trumped Gross Domestic Product, Prime Minister Tshering Tobgay was meditating in his office when his foreign minister entered with news of Trump's global tariffs.

The minister waited patiently for the Prime Minister to complete his meditation—interrupting someone's mindfulness practice in Bhutan was considered roughly equivalent to setting their car on fire in Western nations.

Finally, Tobgay opened his eyes, his expression as calm as the Buddha himself. "You have news from America?" he asked, already knowing the answer through what his staff assumed was either deep political intuition or possibly low-level psychic abilities developed through decades of meditation.

"Yes, Prime Minister. President Trump has imposed a 19% tariff on all Bhutanese exports to the United States."

Tobgay received this information with the same tranquil expression one might use when being told it might drizzle later. In a country where government ministers regularly disappeared for month-long silent retreats, economic catastrophes were treated with a certain philosophical perspective.

"I see," Tobgay nodded thoughtfully. "And what reason has he given for this action?"

The foreign minister consulted his notes. "According to the White House statement, Bhutan has an 'unfair happiness advantage' over America, 'suspiciously intact forests,' and 'too many people wearing robes instead of proper business attire.'"

"Interesting," Tobgay mused, pouring tea for his minister with the mindful attention normally reserved for sacred rituals. "Has the Ministry of Happiness conducted an assessment of this tariff's impact on our GNH index?"

This was a uniquely Bhutanese question. While other nations might immediately calculate GDP impact, currency fluctuations, or stock market reactions, Bhutan's first concern was how the tariffs would affect their internationally renowned Gross National Happiness measurements.

The minister nodded. "The initial assessment suggests a 0.3% reduction in Material Well-being indicators, but a potential 0.5%

increase in Community Vitality as citizens unite against external economic challenges."

"A net happiness gain, then," Tobgay smiled serenely. "Most auspicious."

In the ancient capital of Punakha, where the magnificent dzong monastery-fortress straddled the confluence of two rivers, Bhutan's Economic Advisory Council convened for an emergency meeting that began with twenty minutes of silent meditation—standard protocol for all Bhutanese government functions.

"Trump believes our products have an unfair advantage because they are made with higher consciousness," explained Finance Minister Namgay Tshering, whose economic briefings typically included at least three Buddhist parables. "He specifically mentioned that our textiles are 'suspiciously peaceful-looking' and give American fabrics 'spiritual inferiority complexes.'"

"The American president suffers from attachment to material wealth and aversion to the success of others," observed an elderly monk who served as the council's Spiritual Economics Advisor. "Classic dukkha. Very sad."

The council nodded in unified compassion for Trump's unenlightened state.

Unlike Western nations that might respond to tariffs with retaliatory measures, lobbyist deployments, or frantic market interventions, Bhutan's approach was distinctly... Bhutanese.

"I propose we send President Trump a gift package," suggested the Minister of Mindful Trade Relations. "Traditional Buddhist texts on impermanence, several meditation cushions, and perhaps some of our finest incense."

"And a personal invitation to visit our kingdom," added Tobgay. "Perhaps witnessing our Gross National Happiness measurement system firsthand would help him understand that economic warfare creates suffering for all sentient beings."

The council unanimously approved what they termed a "compassionate non-response response," which would be preceded by three days of special prayers for Trump's spiritual well-being and followed by a nationwide loving-kindness meditation directed toward the American economy.

In the markets of Thimphu, ordinary Bhutanese citizens received news of the tariffs with characteristic equanimity. At a small handicraft shop selling intricately woven textiles and hand-carved wooden phalluses (a traditional symbol of good luck in Bhutan), owner Tashi Wangchuk was explaining the situation to curious tourists.

"Yes, America has decided our happiness is unfair," he chuckled, arranging wooden phalluses by size with the same care a Western shopkeeper might organize fine jewelry. "Perhaps they are right. Is it fair that we measure success by contentment while they chase dollars? Is it fair that our king lives in a modest cottage while their president covers everything in gold?"

He handed a confused American tourist a particularly well-endowed wooden specimen. "Special price. For good luck with your country's trade policies."

In the remote eastern valleys, where some villages remained days of hiking from the nearest road, news of the tariffs spread through Buddhist monasteries via a combination of prayer flags, drum messages, and surprisingly good monastery Wi-Fi. The response was immediate: additional butter lamps were lit for America's economic enlightenment.

Meanwhile in Washington, Trump was explaining his Bhutanese tariff policy with characteristic nuance.

"Bhutan has been very unfair to us on happiness," Trump declared, pointing to a chart comparing American and Bhutanese Gross National Happiness scores. "They have all this happiness, tremendous happiness, and they're not sharing it with America. Very selfish country."

When a reporter pointed out that happiness wasn't an exportable commodity, Trump waved dismissively.

"Then why are they measuring it? Very suspicious. They're clearly hoarding something valuable. Plus, they have all these forests just sitting there making oxygen. American trees should have first priority for photosynthesis rights."

Back in Bhutan, Prime Minister Tobgay composed a personal letter to Trump that exemplified the Bhutanese approach to conflict resolution:

"Dear President Trump,

May this message find you in good health and growing wisdom. We have received news of your tariff on Bhutanese goods with the same acceptance with which we greet both sunshine and rain, for both are necessary parts of life's journey.

Rather than respond with anger, which Buddha teaches us is like drinking poison and expecting the other person to die, we invite you to visit our humble kingdom. Here, you may discover that true wealth lies not in tariff revenues but in the cultivation of compassion.

We have instructed our citizens to include your administration in their daily prayers and will be organizing a special archery tournament in honor of American-Bhutanese friendship.

With boundless loving-kindness,
Tshering Tobgay

P.S. I have included a detailed Tibetan calendar analysis suggesting auspicious dates for removing the tariffs."

As Bhutan's response spread globally, other nations reacting with furious trade wars and diplomatic crises regarded the tiny Himalayan kingdom with a mixture of confusion and reluctant admiration. Leave it to the Bhutanese to respond to economic aggression with meditation cushions and compassion.

In the end, Bhutan's Gross National Happiness actually increased by 1.2% during the "Tariff Crisis"—mostly because citizens reported "deep satisfaction at finally having something interesting to discuss over butter tea."

Chapter 35

The Collectors

Customs and Border Protection's Tariff Nightmare

Two weeks after Trump's sweeping tariffs went into effect, the situation at U.S. Customs and Border Protection headquarters in Washington could most accurately be described as "controlled pandemonium," though the "controlled" part was increasingly debatable.

Acting Commissioner Luis Rodriguez stared in despair at the mounting chaos of his emergency command center. What had once been an orderly conference room now resembled a disaster response unit after the disaster had won.

"Sir," said Deputy Commissioner Janet Chen, approaching with yet another crisis clipboard, "we have a critical calculator shortage."

"A what?" Rodriguez asked, certain he had misheard.

"A calculator shortage, sir. The tariff rates are so specific—17% for Britain, 23% for Puerto Rico, 21.5% for Scotland, 46% for Vietnam—that our agents can't calculate them mentally. They need calculators."

"So order more calculators!" Rodriguez snapped.

Chen sighed. "That's the problem, sir. The government procurement contract for calculators is with Casio. Which is Japanese. Which now has a 24% tariff. Our approved budget can only purchase 40% of the calculators we need."

"Can't we just use phones? Or computers?"

"Technically, yes. But the President specifically ordered that tariff calculations must be done on 'American-made calculating machines.' When informed that America doesn't actually manufacture calculators anymore, he suggested we 'figure it out.'"

Rodriguez massaged his temples. "What about the abacus shortage? Any update?"

"Still critical, sir. The emergency shipment from China is stuck in customs because... well, because we can't calculate the tariff without calculators."

Across the vast operations floor, hundreds of CBP employees were attempting to implement the most complex tariff structure in American history with tools that ranged from inadequate to absurd.

In one corner, a team of agents was using a child's toy cash register to calculate dairy tariffs from Switzerland. In another, a former math teacher had constructed an elaborate slide rule from cafeteria trays and ruler strips.

"Sir!" called out an analyst, "The President just tweeted a tariff adjustment for Madagascar. It's now 47.387% instead of 47%."

"Why the .387?" Rodriguez asked.

"He says it's to account for their 'extra sneaky vanilla tactics' discovered overnight."

Rodriguez turned to his harried legal counsel. "How specific can these tariffs legally get?"

The lawyer, who hadn't slept in 72 hours and was wearing two different shoes, consulted a massive binder. "The regulations don't specify decimal limitations, but our computer systems can only process to two decimal places."

"Then how do we implement a 47.387% tariff?"

The lawyer stared blankly, then whispered, "I think we just round and hope no one notices."

In the port of Los Angeles, the situation was even more dire. Ships sat anchored offshore, unable to unload because the tariff processing system had crashed nationwide. The software, designed in the early 2000s to handle a few dozen tariff categories, had encountered the 437 distinct tariff rates Trump had imposed and promptly committed digital suicide.

CBP officials had resorted to processing imports using a hastily printed "Trump Tariff Bingo Card" system, where countries and products were cross-referenced using colored markers, resulting in a process that one agent described as "kindergarten math meets international trade law."

Back at headquarters, Commissioner Rodriguez was interrupted by another crisis.

"Sir, we have a situation with the tariff stamps," reported the supply officer.

"Tariff stamps? What tariff stamps?"

"The President ordered special 'TARIFFED BY TRUMP' stamps to be applied to all imported goods subject to the new rates. He was very specific about the gold lettering and his signature."

"And the problem is?"

"The stamps were manufactured in Mexico, sir. They're stuck in customs in Laredo because the agents can't calculate the tariff without the calculators that are stuck in customs in Long Beach because they don't have the stamps to mark them as processed."

Rodriguez stared in disbelief. "You're telling me we can't collect tariffs on the tariff stamps we need to mark goods that have paid tariffs?"

"Correct, sir. Also, the stamp ink is from China and the stamp handles are from Vietnam."

At the Canadian border, agents had given up on precision entirely. A leaked internal memo instructed staff to "just collect roughly a quarter of the declared value and put it in the special red box labeled 'WINNING.'"

In Miami, the situation had deteriorated to the point where CBP officers were using an actual Price is Right-style spinning wheel with percentages to determine tariff rates for smaller nations not specifically mentioned in Trump's daily tariff adjustment tweets.

The most surreal scene, however, was at JFK Airport in New York, where a special tariff collection point had been established for passengers returning from abroad. As travelers declared their foreign purchases, agents struggled to apply the correct rates.

"So your Swiss watch has a Japanese movement, Italian leather strap, and was purchased in France?" an agent asked a bewildered traveler. "That's a 19% base tariff, plus 24% for Japan, 18% for Italy, and 20% for France."

"But that adds up to 81%!" protested the traveler.

"No, it's multiplicative, not additive," corrected the agent, before staring hopelessly at his dead calculator. "I think. Maybe. Actually, just give me your watch and we'll mail it back to you once someone figures this out."

The Treasury Department, tasked with actually processing the collected tariff funds, had its own problems. With no standard collection method in place, tariff payments were arriving in various forms: checks, cash, wire transfers, and in one case from a particularly confused importer in Norfolk Island, four live goats.

By the third week, CBP had resorted to using elementary school volunteers for tariff calculations as part of their "arithmetic practice." Third-graders in matching "Junior Tariff Officer" vests could be seen at major ports, diligently multiplying percentages while earning extra credit for their math classes.

White House officials remained oblivious to the implementation nightmare. When presented with evidence that the tariff collection system was on the verge of complete collapse, Trump simply tweeted: "TARIFFS WORKING GREAT! America collecting BILLIONS! Maybe TRILLIONS! Customs doing FANTASTIC job!"

In a final desperate measure, CBP issued emergency "Tariff Approximation Guidelines" authorizing agents to "make your best guess and adjust retroactively if anyone important notices."

As Commissioner Rodriguez surveyed the chaos around him, his deputy approached with yet another clipboard.

"Sir, the President has just announced a new emergency tariff on all abacuses, calculators, and math textbooks coming from 'suspicious math-friendly countries.'"

Rodriguez didn't even look up. "Let me guess: effective immediately, with no implementation guidance, and we need it done by tomorrow?"

"Yes, sir. And there's one more thing..."

"What now?"

"The President wants daily tariff collection totals, but our accountants can't add them up because—"

"—they don't have calculators," Rodriguez finished. "Of course."

Also by Barry Robbins

About the author

B arry Robbins writes books. Quirky books. Books with imagination, with creativity. He can do that because he's retired
and is good at writing quirky, imaginative books, like this one. He's
written six political satires that won three gold medal awards. Well,
no one's perfect. Upon returning from living 12 years in Finland,
where he sharpened his imagination pretending he was on a sunny
beach in January, he moved his attention to books of storytelling.
One gold medal so far. Now he's returned to political satire. He
had to. He just had to. Residing in Florida, he seldom imagines
snow-covered sidewalks.

www.ingramcontent.com/pod-product-compliance
Lightning Source LLC
Chambersburg PA
CBHW061743120626
46550CB00005B/1871